SOUTH EDINBURGH
LIBERTON, SWANSTON, FAIRMILEHEAD
GREENBANK, BLACKFORD, BRAID

PICTORIAL
EDINBURGH
SERIES

Malcolm Cant

SOUTH EDINBURGH

LIBERTON, SWANSTON, FAIRMILEHEAD
GREENBANK, BLACKFORD, BRAID

[signature]

MALCOLM CANT
PUBLICATIONS

To
Brianna in Australia,
my seventh granddaughter

First published in 2007 by
Malcolm Cant Publications
13 Greenbank Row
Edinburgh EH10 5SY

ISBN 10: 0 9552487 0 1
ISBN 13: 978 0 9552487 0 2

British Library Cataloguing-in-Publication Data

A catalogue record for this book is available on request

Book and cover design by Mark Blackadder

Printed and bound by
The Cromwell Press,
Trowbridge, Wiltshire, UK

CONTENTS

BY THE SAME AUTHOR

Marchmont in Edinburgh 1984

Villages of Edinburgh Volume 1 (North) 1986

Villages of Edinburgh Volume 2 (South) 1987

Edinburgh: Sciennes and the Grange 1990

Yerbury: A Photographic Collection 1850-1993 1994

Edinburgh: Gorgie and Dalry 1995

Villages of Edinburgh: An Illustrated Guide Volume 1 (North) 1997

The District of Greenbank in Edinburgh 1998

Villages of Edinburgh: An Illustrated Guide Volume 2 (South) 1999

Old Tollcross, Morningside and Swanston 2001

Marchmont, Sciennes and the Grange 2001

Old Dalry in Edinburgh 2002

Old Gorgie 2002

Edinburgh from the Air: 70 Years of Aerial Photography 2003

Old Dean and Stockbridge 2004

Knowing Your Grandfather 2004

Edinburgh Shops Past and Present 2005

Edinburgh People at Work and Leisure 2006

INTRODUCTION AND ACKNOWLEDGEMENTS

South Edinburgh is divided into four parts with a colour section between Parts 2 and 3. Part 1 deals with Liberton, with an excellent selection of old and new material, covering Kirk Liberton, Liberton Dams, Nether Liberton and Upper or Over Liberton. The early photographs portray those locations as separate hamlets or villages, whereas the more recent pictures show how 'Greater' Liberton came into being. In Part 2 we move westwards from Liberton to look at the very large area of Mortonhall, Swanston, Bowbridge, Lothianburn, Morton Mains, Fairmilehead, Caiystane, Buckstone, Comiston Springs and Oxgangs. This part includes some very interesting photographs by R. A. Rayner, particularly those of Morton Mains.

The colour section is intended to give a topographical spread of all the main areas in the book. The first page reproduces some delightful paintings by well-known artists of the day. These are followed by 1930-style advertisements for houses built by Miller and by Hepburn. Much of the remainder of the colour section is the work of the photographer, Phil Seale, who has also contributed several black/white pictures throughout the book.

Part 3 covers Greenbank, Riselaw, Braidburn, Hermitage, Comiston and Glenlockhart, areas that were dealt with in *The District of Greenbank in Edinburgh* published in 1998. After considerable thought I came to the conclusion that these districts should also appear in the present book. Part 4 encompasses Blackford Hill, Hermitage of Braid and the Braid Hills. This is the shortest section but includes a good selection of pictures of Blackford Pond, golf on the Braids, the Royal Observatory, Braid Bowling Club, Braid Tennis Club and Craigmillar Park Golf Club.

A book of this nature can be put together only with assistance from a great number of people, particularly in the search for suitable photographic material. The nucleus again came from my own collection of Edinburgh photographs. The initial selection was greatly enhanced by several pictures from other collectors. George Fairley and Alan Brotchie contributed very evocative transport scenes, including track-laying equipment for the first trams on Liberton Brae. Alan Brotchie was also instrumental in securing permission from Alastair White to use selected items from his early twentieth-century photographs by R. A. Rayner. The photographs are, in many ways, unsurpassed for conveying the changing topography of well-known Edinburgh locations. In some cases I have included modern equivalents, by Phil Seale, on a 'before and after' basis, such as at Braid Road and Braefoot Terrace. Other early twentieth-century material was provided by Faye and Trevor Yerbury from their Edinburgh archive. Charles Smith, son of the late Charles J. Smith, author and historian, allowed me access to material that was not available from any other source. Almost half of the material used has come from individuals, businesses and institutions who have contributed photographs for specific topics. In each case their names appear after the captions.

I am also indebted to many people for advice and information. In alphabetical order, they are: Eric Anderson; Lois Bain; Alison and Maurice Berrill; Angela and Jim Brass; Dr John Chalmers; Norma and Colin Dale; Lady Elliott; Jim Forson; Eleanor Gilchrist; Dr J. A. Gray;

Margeorie Mekie; Mr & Mrs Menzies; Mrs Mickel; Miss Anne Morham; Rev. John Munro; Cardinal Keith O'Brien; Mr & Mrs Oliphant; John Rennie; Mr & Mrs Richardson; Robin A. Robertson; Rev. Martin Robson; Bryan Ryalls; Mr & Mrs Scott; Robin Sherman; Richard Stenlake; Mrs Anne Stewart; Peter Stubbs; and George Tennant. Several businesses, clubs and national archives also assisted: Braid Bowling Club; Braid Tennis Club; Craigmillar Park Golf Club; Edinburgh City Archives; Edinburgh Room, Central Library; Fairmilehead Parish Church; Greenbank Parish Church; Liberton Golf Club; Liberton Parish Church; Lothianburn Golf Club; Merchants of Edinburgh Golf Club; Mortonhall Golf Club; Nicholas Groves-Raines, Architects; The Royal Observatory; The Royal Scottish Academy; St Fillan's Episcopal Church; Simpson & Brown, Architects; Sisters of the Poor Clares; Swanston Golf Club; and West Lothian Library Services.

After all the photographs had been gathered, and the captions written, the serious business of publication began: Nicola Wood edited the script to her usual high standard; Mark Blackadder brought the basic material to life in the book and cover design; and Oula Jones made everything accessible with a comprehensive index. Without the commitment of those professional people I would not be able to publish my own books.

As always, I thank my wife Phyllis and the members of our ever-increasing extended family for their interest and assistance with numerous tasks.

Malcolm Cant
2007

PART 1

KIRK LIBERTON

LIBERTON DAMS

NETHER LIBERTON

OVER LIBERTON

Liberton is one of the most extensive suburbs on the south side of Edinburgh, encompassing four separate communities of great antiquity. At one time these were separate developments but they have long since been incorporated into what is sometimes referred to, nowadays, as 'Greater' Liberton. The most important, historically, is Kirk Liberton which grew up around the old kirk at the head of Kirk Brae. Two additional communities lie to the north: Liberton Dams nestles at the foot of Liberton Brae; and Nether Liberton is clustered around the junction of Gilmerton Road and Liberton Road. The fourth community, Over Liberton or Upper Liberton, came to prominence through the Littles of Liberton who resided,

firstly, in the defensive Liberton Tower, and, later, in the much more elegant Liberton House. Up until the 1920s the amount of open farm land between those communities was very obvious but successive waves of speculative building gradually created a more homogeneous district. Fortunately this has been achieved without any appreciable loss of Liberton's historical buildings which are probably appreciated and understood better, nowadays, than at certain times in the past.

The origin of the name Liberton is beset with problems. The usual explanation is that it is a corruption of Leperton or Lepertown, from a hospital for lepers which is said to have stood in the district. However, Stuart Harris,

the eminent authority on place names in Edinburgh, states in *The Place Names of Edinburgh* that the leper town explanation 'is not only fanciful but impossible, since the place name is much older than any use of the word "leper" or "lipper" in Scots'. According to the late Mr Harris, the name has an Anglican source in the old words for barley farm on the slope, which would certainly be topographically accurate.

In Part 1, devoted to Liberton, there are 75 illustrations showing the four original communities and many of the streets which now link them together. In this introduction, two early photographs of Edinburgh's tramway era are of particular interest as the city prepares itself again for the new age of the tram. In the pages that follow, Kirk Liberton is dealt with first with a series of pedestrian-friendly street scenes. Liberton Kirk and the Convent of the Poor Clares represent Liberton's strong religious ties. Now that the convent has closed, it is especially important to have a named photograph of the Sisters. On the educational front, two pages are devoted to St Hilda's, the private school for girls; the village school in the 1950s; and, of course, Dr Guthrie's Industrial School. Over the years, Liberton Brae and the adjacent streets have been photographed extensively, often to include aspects of transport. The almost

❧ On Liberton Brae, *c.* 1923, this sturdy dumper truck is off-loading concrete to hold the new tram tracks in place. *Courtesy of A. W. Brotchie.*

deserted side streets contrast noticeably with Liberton Brae which was one of the main tram routes out of Edinburgh. Throughout the book there are several 'before and after' photographs, one of the locations being Braefoot Terrace, where the views are separated by nearly a century. Despite this, the topography is instantly recognisable. Nether Liberton is also included, particularly Good's Corner and the old mill, as well as the much grander Inch House dating from the early seventeenth century. The views of Cameron Toll, Lady Road and Gilmerton Road have changed out of all recognition. The small hamlet of Stenhouse, lying between Lasswade Road and Gilmerton Road, has produced one of the most intriguing pictures in the book, of Margaret Alexander, the Highland dancer and teacher, with her huge collection of medals, cups and trophies.

Over Liberton and the area around Alnwickhill are also included, particularly St

Catherine's House and the ancient well which still remains in the grounds of the Balmwell restaurant. There is also an account of how two of Liberton's most ancient buildings were restored after years of neglect, namely Liberton Tower and Liberton House.

Hopefully some of Liberton's residents will be interested to see the selection of illustrations taken from the sales brochures of Peter Walker & Son who built many of the 1930s houses in and around Orchardhead Road. The final photograph in Part 1 has not been positively identified but perhaps a reader will recognise his or her relation.

✿ This specially decorated tram, at Liberton Cross Roads terminus, was not in normal passenger service. The car was illuminated by 500 electric lamps to advertise the RAF Aircraft and National Services Exhibition by Edinburgh Corporation Transport Department in the Waverley Market in 1939.
Courtesy of A. W. Brotchie.

❧ *Right.* This view, like many others of Liberton, is dominated by the tower of Liberton Parish Church, designed by James Gillespie Graham in 1815. Prior to 1925, Liberton Drive, in the foreground, was part of Kirkgate. The photograph is undated but the railings on the left suggest that house-building on the north side of the Drive had not yet been completed.

❧ *Below right.* Alnwickhill Road, looking north to Arthur's Seat, is largely clear of traffic but is cluttered by a line of telegraph poles, equally as obtrusive, in their day, as modern-day speed cameras. The nearest house on the left, No. 56, now has a conservatory on its south-facing gable, and the bushes on the extreme right of the picture mark the position of Cadogan Road. The street was named in 1926 after the Hon. Victoria Laura Cadogan, daughter of Viscount Chelsea, who married Sir John Little Gilmour of Liberton in 1922. It is difficult to tell what is on the delivery cart as there is a cloth or tarpaulin draped over the horizontal bar.

❧ *Below.* In 1937, when the photograph was produced, this section of Kirkgate was lit by a solitary gas light and all the original iron railings were in position. The very last roof on the left belongs to Liberton Parish Church hall built in 1888 with an imposing wheel window. It was erected partly by public subscription and partly from a grant made by the trustees of the late Miss Anderson of Moredun. *All Malcolm Cant Collection.*

THE CROSS ROADS, LIBERTON.

Kirkgate, Liberton

LIBERTON BRAE.   Edinburgh & Liberton.

✤ *Above.* The east end of Kirkgate, near its junction with Lasswade Road, has a road sign 'SCHOOL – DRIVE SLOWLY'. The building on the corner of Kirkgate and Lasswade Road, now occupied by the Liberton Inn, was once the village school. Between the school building and the road sign was the house of Reuben Butler, immortalised as the schoolmaster in Sir Walter Scott's novel, *The Heart of Midlothian.* A new single-storey school (subsequently extended) was later built in what is now Mount Vernon Road, and Reuben Butler's house became part of the Liberton Inn.

✤ *Above left.* In 1913, when this photograph was produced, Kirk Brae was by no means fully built up, the line of the hedgerows broken only on the right-hand side for house numbers 52, 54 and 56. The other handsome, square house with the conservatory, on the left of the picture, is Craigievar.

✤ *Left.* Liberton Brae was photographed in the same series of pictures which included Kirk Brae shown above. Neither the lady with the parasol, nor the gentleman pushing his bicycle, is concerned about the presence of other traffic. To assist the progress of heavily laden carts on the steep hill, the gradient was specially constructed with smooth, slightly bevelled blocks for the cart wheels and much rougher infill between the tracks to provide a grip for the horses' hooves.
All Malcolm Cant Collection.

❧ *Above right.* Liberton Parish Church and kirkyard, photographed from the west, in 1987. The foundation stone of the building, designed by the eminent architect, James Gillespie Graham, was laid on 27 January 1815, but, strangely, the date of the opening ceremony has never been discovered. The church was built on the site of a much older church which had reached the end of its useful lifetime. Recent research by local historian, John Rennie, has scotched the belief that the old church was damaged by fire. The layout of the church interior has been altered on several occasions over the years (the latest in 2006), resulting in a very light, airy atmosphere which retains its traditional ambience. The kirkyard has some ancient stones including one to William Straiton of Tower Farm, 1754, whose effigy reposes beneath the tablestone.
Photograph by Phyllis M. Cant.

❧ *Right.* According to the Rev. A. Ian Dunlop, author of *The Kirks of Edinburgh*, 'the date of the first [Liberton] manse is unknown but it was described for the Presbytery in 1701'. That building was replaced in 1821, extended in 1880 and used until *c.* 1960. The photograph shows the manse that was in use up until 1960, with the finials of the church in the background. After 1960, a new manse was built in Kirk Park and the old manse was sold.
Malcolm Cant Collection.

❧ *Above.* The bell which hangs in the tower of Liberton Kirk was transferred from the old church when the present church was built in 1815.
Malcolm Cant Collection.

❧ *Left.* The Convent of the Poor Clares, designed by A. E. Purdie of London in 1896, lay on the east side of Lasswade Road just north of Liberton Hospital. The feu charter was dated June 1896 but the Edinburgh community, established in 1895 by eight sisters from the Baddesley Clinton community in Birmingham, did not occupy the building fully until 1902. The photograph shows: the main accommodation with the dormer windows on the left; the priest's house projecting from the gable end; and the chancel and choir with the bellcote on the right. *Malcolm Cant Collection.*

❧ *Below left.* In April 1970, the community of the Poor Clares was photographed by one of their number, Sister Dominic, on the occasion of the Golden Jubilee of Profession of Mother John Furness. Front row, left to right: Sister Mary Francis; Sister Mary Lucy. Second row, left to right: Sister Mary; Sister Mary John; Sister Mary Martha. Group standing at the back, left to right: Sister Mary Gabriel; Sister Mary Felicity; Sister Mary Clare; Sister Mary Teresa; Sister Mary Colette; Sister Mary Bernadette; Sister Mary Andrew; Sister Mary Stephen; Sister Mary Leo; Sister Mary Bernard.
Photograph by Sister Dominic.

❧ *Below.* The photograph shows the interior of the chapel, beyond which is the choir reserved for use by the enclosed sisters only. There is an alabaster figure of the Madonna to the left of the altar and there are two statues against the wall: St Anthony, on the left and St Francis receiving St Clare into the Order, on the right. Between the figure of the Madonna and the doorway, the rectangular shutter on the wall can be opened during Mass so that the enclosed sisters can be present without actually joining members of the public in the chapel.
Photograph by Sister Dominic.

Right. St Hilda's School building, on Kirk Brae, is believed to date from *c.* 1850 with many subsequent alterations. The opening ceremony, in 1901, was conducted by Professor John Kirkpatrick of Edinburgh University. The school, which was confined to resident female pupils only, was divided into four houses – Greeks, Romans, Trojans and Spartans. Several other adjacent buildings were acquired for extra accommodation, including Springwood, St Agnes and Craigievar.
Malcolm Cant Collection.

Below. St Hilda's School was founded by Rosina Gertrude Caroline Stoltz, an honours graduate in classics from Edinburgh University. She married John James Waugh, an Edinburgh solicitor, at St Giles' Cathedral on 11 January 1913. Mrs Waugh continued as head of the school until 1925 when the Waughs moved permanently to Jersey.
From The Story of Saint Hilda's School.

Below right. This 1935 picture at the Anderson Hall in Kirkgate is believed to have been taken at a Halloween party and concert staged by the girls of St Hilda's.

St Hilda's School, Liberton

Left. Car 20 on service No. 7, ready to leave Liberton tram terminus on 18 February 1956. The service was withdrawn on 10 March 1956 and replaced by bus services 7 and 37. To the left of the tram is Liberton Gardens Post Office run by F. McLachlan. The fascia includes 'Library, Stationer, Confectioner and Tobacconist'.
Photograph by M. J. Robertson.
Courtesy of George Fairley.

Below left. Car 23 cruising effortlessly down Liberton Brae, unaffected by lingering pockets of snow.
Photograph by M. J. Robertson.
Courtesy of George Fairley.

Below right. In June 1929 car 349 careered out of control down Liberton Brae and ended up in the garden of No. 40. Fortunately, no-one was seriously injured, and although the tram was badly damaged it was later repaired and returned to service.
Photograph by E. O. Catford.
Courtesy of A. W. Brotchie.

❧ *Above.* The shops, with flats above, were constructed at Braefoot, *c.* 1910. The shop on the extreme left, with J. Ramage & Son on the blind, was occupied as a baker and confectioner which had its depot at No. 60 India Street and branches in Albert Place, West Preston Street, India Street, Princes Street, Leith Walk and Goldenacre Terrace. The next shop, also with a blind, was James B. Baxter, Butcher & Poulterer, and the one to the right of that, A. G. M. Robertson, Stationer & Tobacconist. Two smaller shops are at the right-hand end of the block: A. R. Duguid, the Post Office; and Robert Nicoll, the Chemist. The two horse-drawn vans belong to Ramage & Son and James B. Baxter, respectively.
Malcolm Cant Collection.

❧ *Left.* Almost a century later, 2007, the shop units are extant but the type of business transacted has completely changed.
Photograph by Phil Seale.

❧ *Above left.* The shops referred to on the opposite page are on the left of this 1917 photograph. The corner premises on the right are occupied by H. & T. Moonie, Plumbers & Slaters. *Malcolm Cant Collection.*

❧ *Below left.* Laurie's Map of 1766 shows Liberton Dams between Mayfield Road and Kirk Brae on the main road out of Edinburgh from Causewayside. The cottage to the left of the man with the bicycle is reached by a tiny bridge across the mill lade returning to the Braid Burn.
Photograph by R. A. Rayner. Courtesy of Alastair White.

❧ *Above right.* The photograph is taken at the south end of Mayfield Road looking towards Liberton Brae and Kirk Brae. In the centre of the picture the road narrows to cross the Braid Burn. The sluice gate mechanism can just be seen on the left beside what was Laidlaw's Dairy. *Malcolm Cant Collection.*

❧ *Below right.* This view of Liberton Dams shows its gradual transition from a small country hamlet to an Edinburgh suburb, with houses appearing on Liberton Brae, Kirk Brae and Blackford Glen Road. *Malcolm Cant Collection.*

Right. This group of buildings formed a substantial part of the old community of Nether Liberton. The population probably reached its peak in the late eighteenth century when there were about 300 people. There was a village cross, a weekly market and a school. The two main occupations were brewing and milling, both of which relied heavily upon the water of the Braid Burn which can be seen in the foreground of the picture. The *Edinburgh Advertiser* for 1789 includes an interesting advertisement for the lease of the brewery: 'To let immediately that Brewery at Nether Liberton, Malt Barns etc., containing every requisite for carrying on the business of Brewing and Distilling, having an easy and complete supply of running Water which comes in above the Work: the present Utensils which are in good repair, may be had by agreement.'

Below right. The mill at Nether Liberton took its water supply from the Braid Burn. The timber lade can be seen on the right of the picture, feeding the water to an over-shot iron mill wheel. The spent water ran back into the Braid Burn. Most of the buildings in the picture have survived and are now used for private accommodation.

Below. Two open-topped cable cars at Good's Corner at the car terminus on the corner of Gilmerton Road and Liberton Road.
All Malcolm Cant Collection.

❧ *Above.* The junction of Gilmerton Road and Liberton Road was known for many years as Good's Corner, where the Good family carried on a business of sawmill and joiner's shop. On the right-hand pavement there are two items of street furniture which have long since disappeared: a drinking fountain and a timber shelter used by the cab drivers. *Malcolm Cant Collection.*

❧ *Below left.* The driver and conductor of this cable car pose for a photograph at Nether Liberton before setting off for Pilrig and Leith. The cable car would have been open-topped when first built. *Courtesy of Pat Scoular.*

❧ *Below right.* Looking along Liberton Road towards Liberton Brae from Gordon Terrace, renamed from South Craigmillar Park in 1897. *Malcolm Cant Collection.*

❧ *Above*. Inch House, now a community centre, photographed in 2007. The photograph shows the south-facing frontage with the original house on the right, built in 1617 for James Winram, Keeper of the Great Seal of Scotland. He added a two-storey extension to the north in 1634. The more ornate west wing (on the left of the picture) was added in the late 1700s by the Gilmours who bought the property in 1660. It was the Gilmours who employed the architects, MacGibbon & Ross, to restore the house in 1891, adding the very ornate pilastered porch and pedimented entrance. *Photograph by Phil Seale.*

❧ *Right*. The stone-vaulted dining room on the ground floor of Inch House. *Malcolm Cant Collection.*

❧ *Above left.* Robert Mackinlay, photographed outside the family home at No. 7 Lady Road, ready to travel to his office at the City Exchequer *c.* 1924. The motor cycle is believed to be a Sunbeam, registration number sg 6793, complete with pannier for a briefcase, but in those days it was not usual for the rider to wear protective clothing. *Courtesy of Roger Paton.*

❧ *Below left.* Looking east down Lady Road towards Cameron Toll in 1900. The ground on the right was developed as Cameron Toll Shopping Centre. *Yerbury Collection.*

❧ *Above right.* Car 35 on service No. 7, en route for Liberton, at the junction of Craigmillar Park and Lady Road on 20 February 1954. Tram stop islands were generally confined to the city centre which meant that in the suburbs passengers were obliged to walk out to the trams from the safety of the pavement. Even in 1954 the volume of traffic was beginning to make this dangerous. *Photograph by M. J. Robertson. Courtesy of George Fairley.*

❧ *Below right.* An elegant lamp standard and a water trough protected by three skew stones stood at Cameron Toll at the foot of Dalkeith Road. The entrance to Lady Road is off to the left, obscured by the horse and cart. *Yerbury Collection.*

Right. Kingston, on the west side of Kingston Avenue, was designed in 1867 by Pilkington & Bell for the Edinburgh tailor, William Christie. The original name was Craigend Park. The very grand Gothic structure, in the familiar Pilkington style, has a round stair tower, with a balustrade and a candle-snuffer roof. Part of Liberton Golf Course can be seen on the right. *Malcolm Cant Collection.*

Below. The foundation stone for Liberton Northfield Church was laid in June 1869. The church started as Gilmerton Free following the Disruption in 1843 and, after several changes of name and location, became Liberton Northfield. It is situated on the corner of Gilmerton Road and Mount Vernon Road. *Malcolm Cant Collection.*

Below right. This 1900 photograph of Gilmerton Road includes Kingston, on the left, and Liberton Northfield Church, on the right. *Yerbury Collection.*

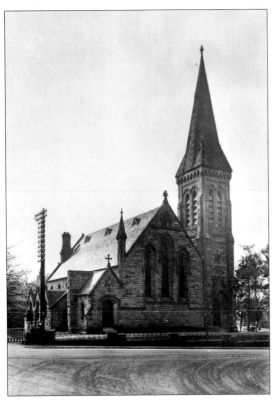

Left. Liberton Golf Club has the privilege of owning one of the most historic clubhouses in Edinburgh. Sunnyside, a medium-sized country house designed by Robert Adam, was built in 1785–8 for Patrick Inglis an Edinburgh merchant. It had a certain elegance about it but suffered from some inconveniences, even by the standards of the late eighteenth century. It had no internal bathrooms and the water supply was from a 50-foot deep well. The Rev. Thomas Whyte, who wrote extensively about the district when he was minister at Liberton Kirk, said in 1789 that: 'It has a splendid portico with a balcony above it. On each side of the portico is a large Venetian window.' Around 1840 the house was purchased and extensively renovated by the Hay family of Duns Castle. They also changed the name from Sunnyside to Kingston Grange, after one of their ancestors, Alexander Seton, who was made Viscount Kingston in 1651. The last person to use Kingston Grange as a private residence was Graham Watson, manager of the Scottish Provident Institution, who leased the property from the Gilmour family. When Mr Watson gave up the house in 1921, the club took over the lease. The photograph shows Kingston Grange, *c.* 1980. *Photograph by Ian Brand. Courtesy of Liberton Golf Club.*

Left. On 9 June 1914 a meeting, attended by over 80 people, was held in Liberton village school to discuss the formation of a local 9-hole golf course. The committee met Colonel Gordon Gilmour on 31 July to discuss the idea of leasing some land but the whole idea was put on hold at the outbreak of the First World War. Talks were restarted in 1919, with the inaugural meeting of the club held in Northfield Church Hall on 19 February 1920. The maximum number of members was fixed at 400 and men and women paid the same fee of 1 guinea for the first year and 2 guineas thereafter. The course was extended to 12 holes in 1920 and 18 holes in 1923. The photograph shows Sir John A. Hope, Bart driving off at the opening of the course on 19 June 1920. *Courtesy of Liberton Golf Club.*

❧ Margaret Leslie Neilson Alexander was born on 2 June 1910 at Ellen's Glen in the village of Stenhouse between Gilmerton Road and Lasswade Road. She married Daniel Thomson on 9 July 1932. The photograph is dated *c.* 1924, by which time the family had moved to Balcarres Street. She won a bewildering number of medals, cups, trophies and rose bowls at various competitions for Highland dancing throughout Scotland. A few items have been passed down to the present family but, sadly, many of the other items were disposed of by Margaret (Peggy) later in life to augment the family budget. *Courtesy of Mrs Margaret Allan, née Thomson.*

BURNBRAE COTTAGE, LIBERTON.

❧ *Above left*. When Alnwickhill filter beds were constructed in 1879 water reached the main reservoir from the Tala, Crawley and Moorfoot pipes and fell by gravity to the slow sand filter beds to purify the water used on the east side of Edinburgh. The lorry is taking away old sand during a regular cleaning procedure in 1987.

❧ *Below left*. When this photograph was taken in 1987, St Catherine's House, in Howdenhall Road, was in a very bad state of repair. Fortunately, it was extensively renovated and opened as a restaurant. The original house, designed by John Simpson for his own use, was built by David Bell in 1806.

❧ *Above right*. This quaint, thatched cottage with the outside stair lay on the south side of Liberton Drive until it was destroyed by fire.

❧ *Below right*. These pieces of broken masonry were fitted together temporarily in 1987 to illustrate how they would have looked as part of the Balm Well of St Katherine (usually spelt with a K), which dates from the fifteenth century. The well was seriously damaged by vandalism but was renovated at the same time as the main house.
All Malcolm Cant Collection.

✤ *Above*. The three illustrations show the fortunes and misfortunes of Liberton Tower over the years: *left*, the tower as depicted in Grant's *Old and New Edinburgh*; *centre*, the tower in 1997 before extensive renovations by the architects, Simpson & Brown; *right*, the tower in 1998, beautifully restored and now in use as holiday accommodation. Liberton Tower stands, surrounded by buildings of considerable antiquity, a few hundred yards north of Liberton Drive, almost opposite the road leading to Meadowhead Farm. It was built in the fifteenth century by the Dalmahoy family who later sold it and the estate to the Little family. Liberton Tower was constructed from two stone vaults, one on top of the other, to create a four-storey rectangular block, thirty-five feet long, twenty-five feet wide and rising forty-five feet to a pitched roof of stone slabs, surrounded by a parapet wall. The construction was harled rubble with dressed stone at the windows. At the time of the 1997 renovations, the two vaults had survived almost intact but some of the timber interior levels had collapsed, revealing a series of corbels which had supported the original timber floor joists. The top vault, which formed the roof, was in remarkably good condition and required only the resetting or replacement of a few slabs. It was then repointed and coated with oil to make it shed water better. A great deal of painstaking research was done to ensure, as far as possible, the integrity of this ancient building. *Modern photographs courtesy of Simpson & Brown, Architects.*

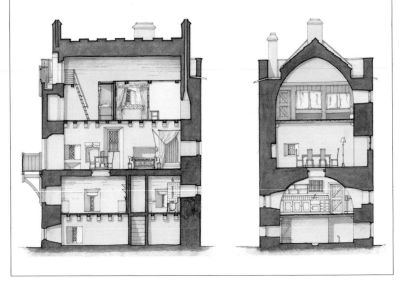

24

❧ *Above, and below left.* Liberton House lies at the end of an avenue of elm trees, a few hundred yards south of Liberton Drive. Its exact age is uncertain although the best-informed opinion places it in the late sixteenth century. It was built for the Littles of Liberton who were until then resident in Liberton Tower. Extensive restoration work was done around 1890 and in 1936. Following serious fire and water damage in 1991, a programme of repair and restoration was started in 1993 by the architects Nicholas Groves-Raines, with assistance from Historic Scotland. The photograph above shows the restored house from the walled garden. *Courtesy of Nicholas Groves-Raines.*

❧ *Above extreme left.* The photograph shows the door to the west extension that is now used as the offices of Nicholas Groves-Raines, Architects. Immediately above the door lintel is the inscription WILLIAME – 1570 – LITIL. *Courtesy of Nicholas Groves-Raines.*

❧ *Above centre.* Like many other houses of its time, Liberton House has a tall lectern-style doocot, probably dating from the late seventeenth century. It is said that the building is haunted by Pierre, a French nobleman, who has 'a propensity to startle visitors by whistling when least expected'. He has not been seen or heard in recent years. *Courtesy of Nicholas Groves-Raines.*

Right. When Peter Walker & Son of No. 53 Buccleuch Street were building houses in Liberton in the early 1930s, they produced an attractive sales brochure which included a map of their various sites. These included Kirk Brae, Lasswade Road, Orchardhead Road, Liberton Brae, Alnwickhill Road and other connecting streets, by then not yet named. The photograph shows the construction of detached bungalows at the south end of Orchardhead Road. No houses have been built on the west side of the road but those on the east are almost ready for occupation. No. 63 is the one with the bay window, nearest to the camera.

Below right. Peter Walker's sales brochure listed the various house types along with specifications, prices and illustrations. The houses shown are, from left to right, Type D; Type C; and Type E, which became Nos 1, 3, 5 & 7 Beauchamp Road.

Below. Naturally, the front cover of the sales brochure issued by Peter Walker & Son, Building Contractors, of No. 53 Buccleuch Street, Edinburgh carried an illustration of one of their best houses. *All Courtesy of Roger Paton.*

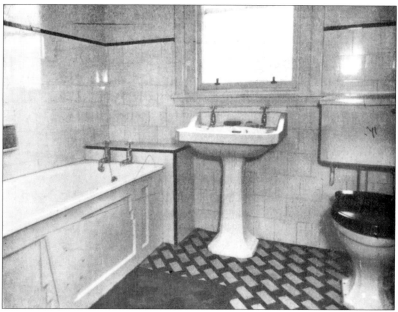

Walker's houses were finished to a high standard, and the show house was furnished in accordance with the latest fashions: *above left*, sitting room with bay window and open coal fire; *above right*, tiled bathroom with low-level cistern and panelled bath; *below left*, dining room with space for easy chairs; *below right*, kitchen with gas cooker, coal or wood-burning stove (probably a Tayco) and what looks like double sinks with a centre fixing for a wringer. *Courtesy of Roger Paton.*

❧ *Above left*. Alexander Walton, the licensed grocer, had branches at No. 27 Lasswade Road and No. 126 Marchmont Road. The photograph shows the Lasswade Road corner premises, *c.* 1945, with, left to right, Nell Walton, David Walton, Chris Kesson, née Walton and Jimmy Reid. Mr Reid started as a message boy with Waltons in 1942 and took over the business in 1976 when David Walton retired. *Courtesy of Miss Lorna Kesson.*

❧ *Above right*. The location of Liberton Dairy and the identity of the proprietor have, unfortunately, not been established. The dentels above the name 'Liberton Dairy' do not match the fascia design of the likely locations at Lasswade Road, Liberton Gardens or Braefoot. *Courtesy of Pat Scoular.*

PART 2

MORTONHALL

SWANSTON

MORTON MAINS

FAIRMILEHEAD

CAIYSTANE

BUCKSTONE

COMISTON SPRINGS

OXGANGS

Part 2 covers a fairly wide geographical area, beginning with Swanston and moving northwards to include Morton Mains, Fairmilehead to Comiston Springs, and then slightly westward to include parts of Oxgangs. There are over 70 illustrations, mostly of a historical nature, but with modern scenes where appropriate.

The early photographs of Swanston show the original thatched cottages at a time when they were occupied by families who worked on the land, either as shepherds or farm labourers. No tractors or other agricultural machinery appear in any of the photographs but a fair amount of manpower and horsepower is obvious. The photograph that is captioned 'Toilers in the Field' shows a group of female workers 'tattie howking'. The women are equipped in the time-honoured way with a sack round their waist like an apron and one corner wrapped round their left forearm to create 'a basket' to hold the potatoes as they make their way along the drill. The Robert Louis Stevenson connection at Swanston Cottage is included. There are also groups of buildings, such as Bowbridge, which Stevenson would have known from his walks in the surrounding countryside. One building he would not have recognised, however, was the Hillburn Roadhouse. The strong agricultural theme is continued at Morton Mains, where there are early photographs by R. A. Rayner, contrasting with modern views of Morton House.

Fairmilehead includes the parish church and much earlier views of the crossroads and Oxgangs Road. At the Princess Margaret Rose Orthopaedic Hospital there is a delightful photograph, among others, of a young patient, Edith Hamilton, on the day that she was visited by the Duke of Kent. Further west, the farm steading, Hunters Tryst, looks distinctly rural compared to its well-ordered appearance now as a restaurant. Nearby, the giant monolith, the Caiy Stane, is believed to be 5,000 years old.

The area in and around Comiston Road, between Fairmilehead and Riselaw, has produced a large number of photographs, beginning with three 1954 pictures of the tramway era. Services 11, 15 and 16 ran to the same terminus at

✄ Mortonhall House in Frogston Road East was built in 1769 for the Trotter family. There are three main floors, plus basement, with a very elegant advanced and pedimented centre. *Photograph by Phil Seale.*

Fairmilehead – apparently regularly and in all weathers. Many readers will recognise the gates and pillars at the north entrance to Braidburn Valley Park; some will also recall the Pentland Hotel at the east end of Camus Avenue; but there will be very few people who can remember when the park gates and pillars were at the entrance to the driveway of Comiston House. The shop development at Buckstone is also depicted in the 1930s, 1950s and the present day.

Before Comiston Road was built, the road south from Morningside Station was Braid Road which had numerous bends and steep inclines. Some idea of what it looked like can be gained from the early twentieth-century pictures near Mortonhall Golf Clubhouse. The road was very narrow and ploughed fields have long since been used for housing development as the city has grown southwards. A brief visual history of St Fillan's Episcopal Church shows the present church in addition to the interior, and the architect's drawing of the first 'tin church',

erected in 1896 on the south corner of Braid Road and Comiston Terrace. St Fillan's in Buckstone Drive was not built until 1938.

Both Comiston Springs and Swanston have been closely involved in the city's early schemes for piping good quality spring water to the wells of the Old Town of Edinburgh. The very first scheme was sanctioned in 1621 by an Act of the old Scottish parliament but it was not until 1672 that the first 3-inch diameter lead pipe was laid all the way from Comiston Springs to Castlehill. The collecting cistern at Comiston Springs shows the lead animals (hare, fox, swan and peewit) which marked the outflow of water from each spring, and another photograph shows the animals in a very different setting. There are also pictures of Comiston Farmhouse (which is extant) and the steadings long since demolished. The Harwells, who also ran the famous tearoom at Colinton, were the last family to farm at Comiston.

The last page of Part 2 has three pictures of the Oxgangs/Colinton Mains district in the 1930s, looking decidedly rural compared to the present day.

❧ At the beginning of the twentieth century, the road to Swanston was little more than a dirt track which suggests that the clean, smartly dressed children probably did not arrive on foot for the photo session.
Photograph by R. A. Rayner.
Courtesy of Alastair White.

❧ *Right.* It is difficult to imagine a more exciting place for a young boy to play than the garden ground of the shepherd's cottage at the top end of the green at Swanston. At the beginning of the twentieth century, this part of Swanston consisted of very basic early eighteenth-century cottages with earth floors and no water or electricity. Piped water was installed in 1934 and electricity in 1949. By the mid-1950s many of the thatched cottages at the top end of the village had fallen into disrepair, and those which were habitable were used only as holiday cottages. Fortunately, Edinburgh Corporation (as it was then) put forward an ambitious scheme in 1956 for the conversion of nine old cottages into seven renovated dwellings. At the present day, as can be seen from the colour photograph on page 60, the cottages are now beautifully maintained.

❧ *Below right.* Thatched cottages exude old-world charm but they do need attention and repair. When the village was being renovated in 1956 the specialised job of thatching was done by John Brough of Auchtermuchty. The larger, two-storey building on the right of the photograph was the school and schoolhouse. Children travelled from as far afield as Bowbridge, Lothianburn, Comiston House, Fordel and Dreghorn. The school closed in 1931 and has been used as a private dwelling ever since.

❧ *Below.* The shepherd's cottage, seen from the south, was built partly into the side of the hill which probably gave it some shelter from the wind but must have made it rather damp.

All Malcolm Cant Collection.

THE SHEPHERDS COTTAGE SWANSTON FROM W. R.R.ARTHUR

THE SHEPHERD'S COTTAGE, SWANSTON.

❧ *Above left.* A young lady tends the stooks of corn in the small field immediately above the village. Most of the men-folk also worked on the land, about fifteen men being needed to work 1,000 acres of sheep, cattle and arable farming. *Courtesy of Mrs Louise Jenkins.*

❧ *Above right.* At Swanston in 1928, it was a very labour-intensive task to build hay ricks or rucks, some of which would stand in the fields until needed. The horse on the right is pulling 'tumblin' Tam', a large timber rake used to draw the hay together. *Malcolm Cant Collection.*

❧ *Below left.* The picture is titled 'Toilers in the Field', and the action is taking place on the east side of the road to Swanston with the farm steadings in the background. *Photograph by R. A. Rayner. Courtesy of Alastair White.*

❧ *Below right.* Three pairs of horses pulling harrows, used to bring the soil to a light tilth ready for sowing. *Malcolm Cant Collection.*

Lothianburn golf course occupies several acres of ground on the lower slopes of Caerketton Hill. The idea of a club in this location was first mooted at a meeting of interested parties under the chairmanship of John Cunningham on 19 July 1893 at No. 5 St Andrew Square. Among those who attended was Gavin Jack, the tenant farmer at Swanston Farm. Later, the first 9-hole course was laid out with the assistance of one of Gavin Jack's employees, William Laidlaw, who later became the club's first greenkeeper. A modest clubhouse was built in 1896 and in 1899 the course was extended to eighteen holes. A more substantial clubhouse was built by James Millar of Morningside and opened by Major Trotter on 24 September 1910. In 1928 the course was redesigned by James Braid and in 1931 the club's most renowned player, Tommy Armour, won the British Open Championship at Carnoustie. The history of the club was written by William Pritchard, OBE in *Lothianburn Golf Club Centenary 1893–1993*. The photograph shows the clubhouse as extended and renovated in 1994. *Photograph by Phil Seale.*

Hillend Park was gifted to the city by John White, an Edinburgh builder, and opened to the public by Lord Provost Sir William Sleigh in July 1924. Since then the growth of Edinburgh has brought the southern suburbs almost to the base of the Pentland Hills. Of all the outdoor activities at Hillend, ski-ing is probably the most popular. The potential was recognised as long ago as 1964 by G. Boyd Anderson, an Edinburgh businessman, whose enthusiasm and financial backing brought ski-ing to Hillend. The original fifty-metre experimental slope, laid in 1964, was resited and extended in 1965, and, in the following year, a double chairlift of 360 metres was installed. The complex, which cost £40,000, was officially opened on 1 October 1966 by Lord Provost Herbert Brechin, which was followed by a special open slalom competition for the Dendix Snowslope Trophy.

As can be seen from this 2007 photograph, the facilities available at Hillend have been extended in recent years. *Photograph by Phil Seale.*

Swanston Golf Course is laid out on the lower slopes of Caerketton Hill, to the west of the village, the first hole, appropriately named RLS, running parallel to the garden of Swanston Cottage. The club was formed in 1927 by Miss Margaret Carswell who was also a prominent member of the Edinburgh Women's Athletic Club. Finding it almost impossible to obtain sufficient places for ladies in local golf clubs (although Lothianburn had admitted ladies since 1907), Miss Carswell decided to found and construct her own course, solely for the use of female members. With the assistance of Herbert More of the Merchants of Edinburgh Golf Club, she proceeded to lay out a 9-hole course. True to her original concept, Miss Carswell insisted that membership be confined to ladies only, although this rule was eventually relaxed.

At the present day, Swanston's 18-hole course is a par 66, played over 5,004 yards, the course record of 58 having been set by 25-year old John Gallagher on 14 June 2006. However, following the opening of the new clubhouse in 2007, there are plans to make substantial changes to the course, which will increase the overall length to 5,557 yards, par 68. The idea is to create six new holes, on lower ground to the north, to replace six of the steeper holes of the original course. The plans will also include a new 9-hole short course for beginners. The photograph above, taken in 2007, shows a group on the green of the fifteenth hole, the Hill o' Hame. *Photograph by Phil Seale.*

Left. The photograph was taken at Swanston in the garden of Rathillet on 13 October 1952. From left to right: Herbert More of Swanston Golf Club; Miss Margaret Carswell, founder of Swanston Golf Club; and Eric McRuvie, the well-known golfer of the 1930s, from Elie in Fife. The seat has a plaque 'In Appreciation of Herbert More 1927–1952, to mark twenty-five years at Swanston Golf Club. *Courtesy of Ellen and Jim McLagan.*

Right. In 1758 Edinburgh Town Council secured an Act of Parliament to enable them to use spring water from Swanston, to augment the existing supply from Comiston. The landowner, Henry Trotter, objected but he lost his appeal, both in the Court of Session and the House of Lords. Following the court case, a water-house and filter beds were erected to the west of the village. After the water-house was built in 1761 the city fathers decided that additional accommodation, in the form of a small single-storey thatched cottage, was needed as a general meeting place. This small cottage was greatly enlarged around 1835 when the magistrates added a second storey and replaced the thatch with slate. Bow windows were built out at the front and a single-storey addition was constructed to the east. By far the most interesting era at Swanston, however, began in 1867 when Thomas Stevenson, father of Robert Louis Stevenson, took the tenancy of the house as a summer retreat. The photograph shows Swanston Cottage in 2000. *Photograph by Phil Seale.*

Below left. Robert Lewis Balfour Stevenson was born in Edinburgh on 13 November 1850. On his father's side the family had a long tradition of designing and building lighthouses. Louis' mother was Margaret Balfour whose father was the Rev. Lewis Balfour of Colinton Parish Church. The Stevensons lived at Howard Place, Inverleith Terrace and Heriot Row. They also held the tenancy of Swanston Cottage from 1867 to 1880, during which time Stevenson made frequent use of this quiet country retreat to write his many novels and poems. When his father died in 1887, Stevenson visited Edinburgh for the last time. He spent the rest of his life, firstly in America, and then in Samoa where he died on 3 December 1894. The photograph shows Stevenson as an advocate of the Scottish Bar to which he was admitted in 1875. *From* Robert Louis Stevenson's Edinburgh.

Below right. Stevenson's nurse was Alison Cunningham, or 'Cummy' to whom he dedicated *A Child's Garden of Verses*. After the Stevensons left Swanston, Cummy remained behind with her brother who was the waterman. She moved to Balcarres Street in 1893 and later to Comiston Place where she died on 21 July 1913 at the age of 91. *Malcolm Cant Collection.*

Left. This 1953 photograph shows the farmhouse and part of the steadings of Bowbridge Farm. According to *The Place Names of Edinburgh* by Stuart Harris, Bowbridge can be traced to the sixteenth century as *Bowbrig*, describing a stone-arched bridge over the Swanston Burn. The bridge lay on the east side of Biggar Road a few hundred yards south of what was the Hillburn Roadhouse. The farmhouse was also on the east side, a short distance south of the bridge. All of Bowbridge was demolished for the construction of the Edinburgh City Bypass. *Photograph by H. D. Wylie. © Edinburgh City Libraries. All rights reserved.*

Below left. This picture postcard, posted on 9 October 1911, shows the old thatched cottage at Lothianburn which was used for a while by the greenkeeper at Lothianburn Golf Club. The clubhouse, opened in 1910, can be seen on the left. *Malcolm Cant Collection.*

Below. Fairmilehead Cottage lay on the north side of Oxgangs Road near the junction with Fairmile Avenue. Its position can be judged from the photograph of the crossroads at Fairmilehead which appears on page 45. The cottage was probably demolished in the early 1930s in anticipation of house-building on the north side of Oxgangs Road. *Photograph by R. A. Rayner. Courtesy of Alastair White.*

❧ *Above.* The Hillburn Roadhouse, now the Fairmile Inn, was designed by T. Bowhill Gibson in 1938, in the Art Deco style of the period. His other commissions in Edinburgh included: the County Cinema in Portobello; the County Cinema in Craigmillar; and the Dominion Cinema in Morningside. When the Hillburn was opened at Lothianburn, its windows and balconies had a panoramic view of Swanston village and the Pentland Hills. Although the idea of a city bypass dates from about the same period, it was a long time before serious thought was given actually to building it.

❧ *Left.* The photograph shows Nellie and John M. Oman in the Isle of Man in 1937, the year before they opened the Hillburn Roadhouse. John McLennan Oman was born in 1877 in Caithness, the eldest son of Alexander Oman, a flagstone dresser, and Diana McLennan, whose father was a grocer. The Oman family relocated to Edinburgh, *c.* 1890, where Johnny worked in public houses as a barman. Helen (Nellie) Lavin was born in 1875 in the Grassmarket in Edinburgh, the eldest daughter of an immigrant Irish labourer from County Leitrim, Patrick Lavin, and his wife, Maggie Ferguson, born in Banffshire. Johnny and Nellie married in 1899 and initially lived in Home Street. In 1921 they bought their first pub, the Palace Arms, at the foot of the Royal Mile, followed by the Meadow Bar in Buccleuch Street, and then the Duddingston Arms, which is now called Oman's. Their most ambitious project was, however, to build the Hillburn Roadhouse which was opened in 1938. After Johnny died of a heart attack in 1942, Nellie took over the business while living in the house above the roadhouse. She eventually sold the business to Scottish Brewers and retired in 1956 to a house at No. 39 Grange Road where she died, aged 89, in 1964. Sadly, they lost a daughter, aged 8, and a son, aged 28, to illness. *Both photographs courtesy of Colin Dale.*

❧ *Above.* The press announcement for the opening of the Hillburn Roadhouse on Friday 19 August 1938 promised a completely new experience – for the growing number of car-owning families! *Courtesy of Colin Dale.*

❧ *Above left.* The photograph shows the curved bar and distinctive 1930s style of furnishings at the Hillburn Roadhouse when it opened in 1938. The opening was given fairly extensive, same-day coverage by *The Evening Dispatch* from which it was evident that the leading dignitaries took the opportunity to score points against the anti-drink lobby of the day. Baillie J. R. Coltart, presiding at the dinner given by Mr Oman, wished the venture well and said that he hoped 'that the trade would fight those people who were wanting to filch away their liberties'. He went on to say that he thought that the people who were out to abolish drink would change their minds if they were shown over the premises. *Courtesy of the Royal Incorporation of Architects in Scotland and the Royal Commission on the Ancient and Historical Monuments of Scotland.*

❧ *Left.* The skittle alley at the Hillburn Roadhouse was one of the main attractions when it was first built, and remained a popular venue for many years thereafter. The prominent advertisements for William Younger's Beer suggest that the brewery had some form of financial involvement. The alley was located in the basement where there were also facilities for darts and a lounge bar for the patrons. The ground floor had the restaurant, the main bar and lounge and a separate cocktail bar, while the top floor was laid out as a flat for the use of the manager, Tom Ward, who had previously managed one of Mr Oman's other hostelries, the Duddingston Arms. *Courtesy of the Royal Incorporation of Architects in Scotland and the Royal Commission on the Ancient and Historical Monuments of Scotland.*

Right. The woman leading the horse and cart is passing the twin ivy-covered pavilions at the entrance to Morton House. The right-hand pavilion roof was altered from pitched to ogee in the late 1960s to conform to the original design. The semi-detached cottages date from before 1842. The left-hand cottage is Mary's Cottage named after Mary Young, 'the pig-wife', who lived there during her employment by the farm manager, Jim Brass, until her death in 1989, aged 70. Behind the trees on the right is the former church hall, a small, single-storey building of uncertain date in which there was a fireplace, pews and a tiny vestry. To the east is Morton Mains Farmhouse, *c.* 1840, and the steadings, at least a century earlier.

Below. The boys carrying the pitchers are walking towards Faimilehead on what is now Frogston Road West, near its junction with Winton Drive. The thatched cottage in the centre of the picture is named 'The Luggie' (a small cottage) on the 1932 Ordnance Survey map. The narrow driveway in front of the cottage became Winton Drive.

Below right. Two pairs of working horses coming in from the fields at Morton Mains Farm. The line of the Biggar road can just be seen to the left of the big tree, and the white gable ends of Bowbridge (already referred to) are between the two small trees. *All photographs by R. A. Rayner. Courtesy of Alastair White.*

Left. Morton House stands in several acres of mature garden at the east end of Winton Loan. It consists of two distinctly different styles of architecture, designed about a century apart. The older part, seen here, of two main storeys and an attic, has a central chimney gable flanked by half-dormers on each side. The southmost dormer has the date 1702 when this part of the house was built by Thomas Rigg, Deputy Sheriff of Edinburgh.

Below left. In 1806 a completely new block of elegant Georgian symmetry was built in contrast to the style of the original house. Its central Roman Doric doorway, with supporting small-pane windows, is flanked by much broader windows lighting the principal rooms. The whole façade is set off against a sweeping carriageway between rusticated gate piers with urns.

Below. The Belvedere, to the south-east of the house, dates from the early eighteenth century. It is two storeys in height with a pitched roof and large windows in the upper storey. It is reputed to have been used by the menfolk of the house as a retreat, prompting the Rev. Thomas Whyte to observe in 1792 that 'the Belvedere is mightily well situated'. *All photographs by Phyllis M. Cant.*

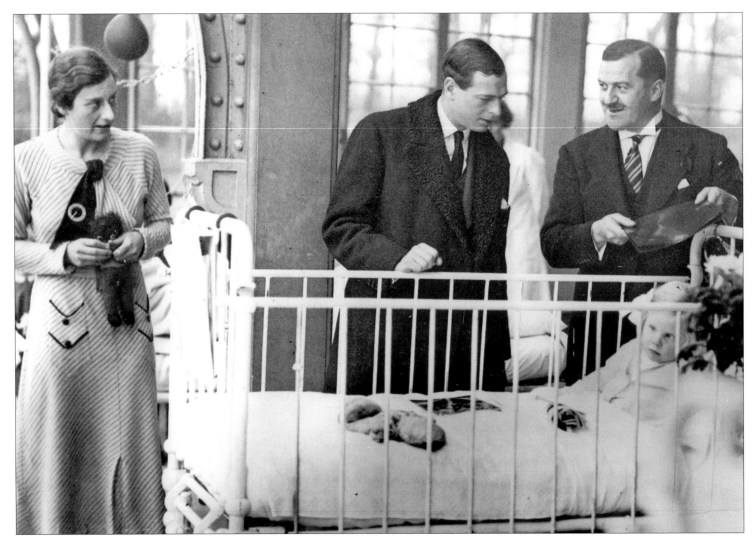

Edith Hamilton, aged 2, is probably too young to feel apprehensive about the outcome of this high-level consultation at the Princess Margaret Rose Orthopaedic Hospital in 1933. The consultant, William Alexander Cochrane, is showing the patient's X-rays to the Duke of Kent during one of his visits to the hospital. Mr Cochrane was appointed as the first consultant at the PMR at the age of 37. His early career included service as a Captain in the Royal Army Medical Corps during the First World War, and at the Edinburgh War Hospital at Bangour, before taking up a senior position at the Massachusetts General Hospital, Boston. On his return to Edinburgh he was appointed Honorary Assistant Surgeon at the Royal Infirmary of Edinburgh and then consultant at the Princess Margaret Rose Orthopaedic Hospital.

The lady on the left of the photograph is Margaret Harper who qualified as a Froebel teacher from St George's Training College and was employed at the hospital to teach those children who were unable to attend school. In 1935 she married William James Kinloch Anderson of William Anderson & Sons, Kiltmakers and Outfitters, in George Street. *Courtesy of Mrs Edith M. Macaskill, née Hamilton.*

❧ *Above left.* The photograph shows the layout of the Princess Margaret Rose Orthopaedic Hospital shortly after it was opened in 1932. The nurses' home is in the top left-hand corner, to the right of which is the laundry. Three pavilion-style wards face south to Frogston Road West, and the administration and theatre buildings lie between the wards and the laundry.

❧ *Above right.* By the late 1950s the hospital was considerably enlarged by two additional pavilion wards and, to the right, the double-storey wards 6 to 9. Along the east boundary is the Clinical Research Unit commissioned in the early 1960s. *Courtesy of Michael Devlin.*

❧ *Below left.* Ward 3 was a children's ward, photographed shortly after the Second World War. The tilted beds were to allow traction for the treatment of hip dysplasia and Perthes' disease which both affect the head of the femur.

❧ *Below right.* The pool, constructed in 1936, was used in connection with the physiotherapy department. It was still in use in the mid-1980s.

❧ The Princess Margaret Rose Orthopaedic Hospital became pre-eminent in the United Kingdom over the 70 years of its life for two main reasons: firstly, it encouraged its orthopaedic surgeons to subspecialise, so that highly developed units evolved in paediatric, spinal, upper limb, arthroplasty (artificial joint replacement) and trauma surgery, the last being based at the Royal Infirmary orthopaedic wards; and secondly, the hospital then attracted international trainees and dedicated teams of nurses, physiotherapists, occupational therapists, prosthetists and radiographers. The splendid setting of the hospital and its enlightened approach to musculoskeletal conditions ensured that the 'PMR' was regarded as a centre of excellence throughout the world.
Photographs courtesy of Mr Malcolm Macnicol.

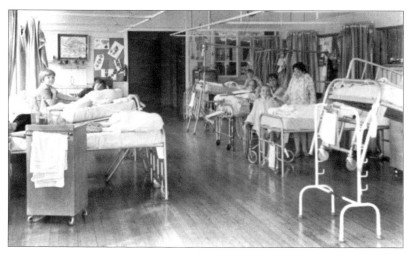

❧ Fairmilehead Parish Church, on the corner of Buckstone Terrace and Frogston Road West, was designed in 1937 by the architect, L. Grahame Thomson. It was built of Craigmillar stone with door and window facings of Doddington stone, and the interior woodwork was by Scott Morton & Co., of Murieston. The bell came from St Aidan's, Montrose. The stained glass includes four works by William Wilson and also three works by the Abbey Studio entitled: The Pure in Heart; Light of the World; and David and Jonathon. The interior of the church was completely renovated during 2006 when the organ was also relocated and rebuilt. To the right of the main church building is the original session room, now used as the church office. The taller building with the curved, glazed gable is the 1997 Caerketton Hall, and the flat roofed building is the Frogston Hall built in 1966 and remodelled in 1997. *Photograph by Phil Seale*

Fairmilehead, Edinburgh.

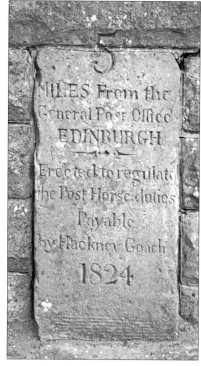

Left. This 1906 view of the crossroads at Fairmilehead is taken from Frogston Road West looking towards Oxgangs Road where Fairmilehead Cottage can just be seen on the brow of the hill. *Malcolm Cant Collection.*

Below left. Fairmilehead Cottage is seen at closer range in this 1904 photograph of Oxgangs Road. *Malcolm Cant Collection.*

Below centre. The photograph is captioned 'Post Coach Mile Stone, Near Oxgangs. Aug. 1929', but the stone has clearly been neglected and allowed to become almost indecipherable. *Malcolm Cant Collection.*

Below right. At the present day the milestone is set into a garden wall in Oxgangs Road and has obviously been re-cut since 1929. The top has, unfortunately, been slightly damaged in an effort to align it with the stonework of the garden wall. Regulations for Hackney Coaches, 1824, fixed the fare at one shilling for half a mile or for thirty minutes. The coachman had the option to charge by distance or by time, but not both. *Photograph by Phil Seale.*

Right. Hunters Tryst at the west end of Oxgangs Road dates from about 1800. It is shown by that name on Knox's map of 1812, displacing a previous name, Sourhole. When the present Hunters Tryst building was called Sourhole, the *name* Hunters Tryst was applied to a completely different hostelry a short distance to the south of Fairmilehead. It is not known whether the name, Hunter, describes the clientele or was the name of the proprietor. In the early nineteenth century it was the meeting place of the Six Foot High Club which included many of Edinburgh's distinguished literary figures, including Sir Walter Scott, James Hogg, J. G. Lockhart and Christopher North. Membership was confined to males over six feet in height, but exceptions were made for honorary members of sufficient stature in their chosen field. *Courtesy of Charles J. Smith's family.*

Below centre. The photograph, *c.* 1898, shows the Caiy Stane, from the east, surrounded by open farmland: the stone now stands in a semi-circular recess off the east pavement in Caiystane View. The information board erected by the National Trust for Scotland states that the stone may have been erected as early as the Neolithic period, possibly before 3000 B.C., to denote a ritual or burial place. The stone, in its modern setting, is shown on page 64. *Courtesy of Charles J. Smith's family.*

Below right. This milestone, clearly showing the number 3, is set into the boundary wall, a few hundred yards north of the Fairmilehead junction. The remainder of the inscription on the stone has become indecipherable. Normally the mileage was measured from the General Post Office in Waterloo Place but in this case it has obviously been taken from Tollcross, similar to the existing stone on the west side of Morningside Road, opposite the Bore Stone. *Courtesy of Charles J. Smith's family.*

Left. Car 364 on service No. 15 already has its destination board changed to King's Road although it has not yet reached the Fairmilehead terminus, on 18 September 1954. The advertisement on the side of the tram for 'Weston's Quality Biscuits' also appears on the following tram on service No. 11. The tram stop, near the junction with Buckstone Avenue, has a sign 'CARS FROM TOWN STOP HERE', and there is also a stop sign for the No. 15 bus, newly erected for the changeover from trams to buses the following day.

Below left. Car 217 on service No. 11 at the Fairmilehead terminus on 18 September 1954 has been prepared for the return journey to Stanley Road. The advertisement is 'Ask for Smith's Bread & Cakes'. The two trams in the background are waiting for Car 217 to use the crossover track so that they can move up to the terminus.

Below right. A light fall of snow on 30 January 1954 has not impeded the progress of Car 267 on service No. 16 bound for Fairmilehead. The advertisement is 'schweppervescence, lasts the whole drink through'. The photograph was taken on the Buckstone Terrace section of Comiston Road, near the junction with Caiystane Crescent.
All courtesy of George Fairley.

Below. Comiston House, at the west end of Camus Avenue, was built in 1815 for Sir James Forrest, Lord Provost of Edinburgh from 1838 to 1843. The name Comiston is of some antiquity being recorded as early as the fourteenth century and shown on Adair's map of 1682 as Comeston. The estate was first bought by the Forrest family in 1715, a century before Sir James built the present house. After the Forrest baronetcy became extinct in 1928, the house was used as the Pentland Hotel but in the late 1980s it was unoccupied and boarded up. Fortunately, it was rescued and is now beautifully restored as private housing. *Photograph by Joyce Wallace.*

Right. When Comiston House was built it was approached by a very long driveway from Comiston Road, where there was a lodge house and gates. The photograph shows W. E. Evans with his camera at the gates which have been moved on two occasions. Edinburgh City Archives hold drawings, dated 9 February 1923, to widen Comiston Road and reposition the gates to the north-west. It was also necessary to move the wash house from the east side of the lodge to the south. Presumably they took the opportunity to reposition 'the privy' which is shown in the plans in the middle of the new pavement. *Courtesy of Charles Smith's family and G. Anderson.*

Below right. The gates and gate piers were moved in the mid-1930s to their present position at the north entrance to Braidburn Valley Park. *Photograph by W. R. Smith.*

🦋 *Above left.* This undated picture postcard does not say 'Within a Mile' of what, but clearly the view is of the junction of Braid Road (on the right) and Buckstone Terrace (on the left) almost opposite the shops shown on this page. *Malcolm Cant Collection.*

🦋 *Below left.* On 30 January 1954, Car 208 on service No. 16 glides to a halt at the tram stop beside the British Linen Bank. A prospective passenger has already stepped out from the pavement. *Photograph by George Fairley.*

🦋 *Above right.* The shops and flats were built by James Miller & Partners Ltd, of Edinburgh in the mid-1930s. The corner premises, occupied by the British Linen Bank, are listed in the *Edinburgh & Leith Post Office Directory* for 1937. Other shops included: Thomson's Newsagent at No. 4; P. Thomson, the fruiterer, at No. 8; the Edinburgh & Dumfriesshire Dairy Co. at No. 10; and Wm Adams, the chemist, at No. 12. *Courtesy of Mrs Pauline McNaught and Mrs Maria McCallum.*

🦋 *Below right.* Approximately 70 years later, the corner premises are occupied by the Bank of Scotland (which amalgamated with the British Linen Bank in 1971), and the other shops are still serving the community well. *Photograph by Phil Seale.*

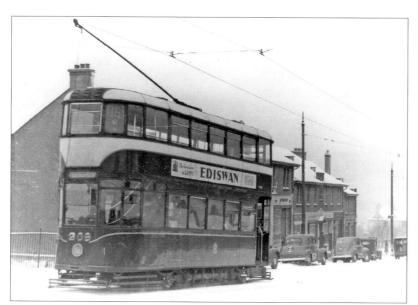

☘ *Above.* Braid Road was a very narrow country road when this photograph was taken, probably *c.* 1910. Mortonhall Golf Clubhouse, on the right, was designed in 1892 by the architect, Sydney Mitchell, who was also commissioned to enlarge it by the addition of another floor in 1903. The large, detached house on the left is Braehead dating from the early twentieth century. The original plans for the house, dated July 1905, have survived but were not signed by the architect. His address is, however, included, namely No. 7 Young Street which was the office of Archibald Macpherson who did work for the Roman Catholic church at St Catherine's Convent at Lauriston and St Margaret's Convent at Greenhill. For a few years after 1905, Archibald Macpherson's home address is given as Braehead Cottage, Old Braid Road, which suggests that he probably designed the house, initially for his own use. In the mid-1930s, Braehead was the home of the Danish Consul, Erik Schacke, a produce broker, whose business address was No. 60a Constitution Street. *Photograph by R. A. Rayner. Courtesy of Alastair White.*

☘ *Right.* A century later, the same section of roadway is much wider, alterations have been made to the clubhouse, and the ploughed field is now occupied by houses and gardens. *Photograph by Phil Seale.*

Left. This view of Braid Road, probably taken at the same time as the view of Mortonhall Golf Clubhouse, shows Buckstone farmhouse and numerous outbuildings to the right of the girl with the bicycle. At the present day, several of the outbuildings have been demolished but the farmhouse has been beautifully restored as a private house. *Photograph by R. A. Rayner. Courtesy of Alastair White.*

Below left. This view, in 2007, shows Braid Road considerably widened and many of the trees cleared from the left-hand side of the road. The square building with the pitched roof nearest to the camera is the garage for Buckstone farmhouse. The Buck Stane is situated in the recessed entrance. *Photograph by Phil Seale.*

Below. The Buck Stane stands off the east pavement of Braid Road a few hundred yards north of the junction with Buckstone Drive. *Photograph by Phil Seale.*

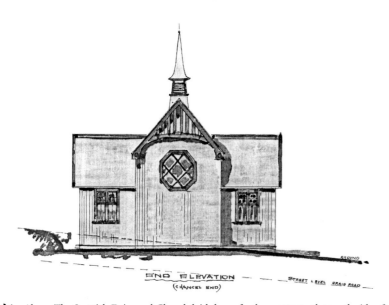

❧ *Above.* The Scottish Episcopal Church laid down further roots on the south side of Edinburgh in 1874 when a prospective congregation met on 30 August in the Drill Hall of Merchiston Castle School, later occupied by Napier University. Shortly thereafter a decision was taken to build a permanent church, designed by the architect, Hippolyte Blanc. The completed building, Christ Church at Holy Corner, was opened on 4 June 1876. As Morningside developed south of the suburban railway, Christ Church appointed its first curate, in 1893, to take services at the Morningside Hall in Morningside Drive. By 1896 the members had increased sufficiently to consider a more permanent home, and a site was acquired on the south corner of Braid Road and Comiston Terrace for the first St Fillan's. The original drawings for the building, which came to be known as 'the tin kirk', have survived. They were drawn up by Messrs Speirs & Co., Iron Building Contractors, No. 125 West Regent Street, Glasgow and approved by the Dean of Guild Court on 20 February 1896. The ground plan shows the chancel, vestry, choir vestry and central aisle. The above illustration shows the east elevation with the distinctive octagonal window. *Courtesy of Edinburgh City Archivist.*

❧ *Above right.* Rather remarkably, a photograph of the interior of 'the tin kirk', showing the octagonal window, has also survived, taken at the Harvest Festival in 1900. The first church closed in 1906 as the ground was required for house-building, but, in fact, the site was not developed until 1922 when Hunter's Garage was built. *Courtesy of St Fillan's Episcopal Church.*

❧ *Right.* The second St Fillan's Church was opened in Buckstone Drive in 1938 after other sites had been rejected. The building was dedicated on 30 March 1940 by the Bishop of Edinburgh, Arthur John Maclean. It became an independent congregation in 1970 and an incumbency in 1978. In 1977 St Fillan's was linked to St Hilda's in Oxgangs Avenue, which has now closed. *Photograph by Phil Seale.*

❧ *Left.* Mrs Betty Millar, the Newhaven fishwife, attracted a lot of attention and good custom from the residents around Riselaw and Buckstone. Her unofficial open-air stance was on the corner of Riselaw Crescent and Comiston Road. Newhaven was for many years the centre of a busy fishing industry until its gradual demise from the 1960s. Like many fishing villages in Scotland, most families had some connection with the industry. Fathers and sons went to sea and mothers and daughters helped with the nets and lines. Many of the womenfolk also worked as fishwives selling fish direct to housewives in most districts of Edinburgh. *Photograph by W. R. Smith.*

❧ *Below.* This wintry scene shows Thomas Robert McIlwrick of No. 50 Greenbank Crescent out for his usual constitutional. The photograph is taken at the junction of Comiston Rise and Comiston Road in the 1920s, with the Braid Hills in the background. Part of Braid Road and Mortonhall Golf Clubhouse can be seen to the right of centre. The house immediately behind Mr McIlwrick, called 'The Whins', was built in the 1920s by Gibson Martin for Graham Menzies, FRICS. The photograph shows the rear of the house, the entrance being from Buckstane Park. Mr McIlwrick was a keen member of the Merchants Golf Club, and became a director and secretary of J. & R. Allan's in South Bridge. *Courtesy of the McIlwrick Family.*

Above right. The photograph shows the interior of the collecting cistern which still exists to the south of Oxgangs Avenue. The lead animals (hare, fox, swan and peewit), which marked the outflow of each spring, are now in the Museum of Edinburgh in the Canongate. In 1621 an Act of the old Scottish parliament was passed to enable Edinburgh to bring water for public consumption from the springs at Comiston to Castlehill. The idea of a gravity-fed system was devised by George Sinclare and the contract (delayed until 1672) to lay a 3-inch diameter lead pipe was placed with a German engineer by the name of Peter Brauss or Bruschi. Sinclare had calculated that Comiston was about 60 feet higher than the intended collecting tank at Castlehill. To begin with, one spring only was used but this was later increased to four. In 1720 the 3-inch diameter pipe was replaced by a 5-inch pipe which greatly increased the volume of water reaching the Old Town wells.
From The Water Supply of Edinburgh.

Above. Children from Greenbank Church Sunday School had the opportunity to see the hare and the swan at close range before the lead animals were placed in what was then Huntly House Museum.
Courtesy of Greenbank Parish Church.

Right. Hay-making was a labour-intensive job in the 1950s. At Comiston Farm with Caerketton Hill in the background, the man in the centre is operating a horse-drawn hay-sweep which drew the hay into large heaps that were then built into ricks or rucks. *Photograph by Peter F. Riddell.*

❧ *Left.* Comiston farmhouse, photographed *c.* 1947, is a large, square, stone building of uncertain date which stands among mature trees to the west of Pentland View. It is no longer a farmhouse and the surrounding farm land has long since been absorbed by urban development. The farm steadings and farm labourers' cottages, now demolished, lay to the north, on the sloping ground between the farmhouse and the Braid Burn. William Wilkie was the tenant farmer at Braid Farm and also had responsibility for Comiston Farm between 1925 and 1937. In 1938 George and Elizabeth Harwell took over the tenancy and lived in the farmhouse until 1978. They also owned Harwells of Colinton, the stationer, baker and tearoom in Bridge Road, Colinton.

❧ *Below left.* This aerial view, *c.* 1947, shows the greenhouses and steadings of Comiston Farm, looking north to the houses of Greenbank Road, Rise and Crescent. The collecting cistern for Comiston Springs is the small building with the pitched roof in the top right-hand corner of the photograph.

❧ *Below.* This photograph is taken slightly to the east of the previous one. It shows the houses of Pentland Gardens in the top right-hand corner. The path was part of Cockmylane which had a right of way through the farm steadings.
All courtesy of George G. Harwell.

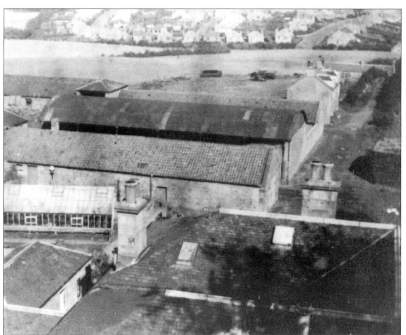

Below. Graham Moonie on the path between Oxgangs farmhouse and Redford Road in 1935. Oxgangs Farm Drive was built along the approximate line of the pathway that joined Redford Road nearly opposite Fordel. An early photograph of Fordel shows only three houses: Fordel Cottage, at one time the gamekeeper's house for the Dreghorn estate; a cottage used as a military post office during the First World War; and a smaller thatched cottage used by an estate gardener. The last vestige of this small hamlet was Fordel Cottage demolished in 1985 shortly after the construction of the City Bypass.
Courtesy of Graham Moonie.

Top. The roofs of Oxgangs farmhouse and steadings can just be seen behind the row of haystacks in this 1933 photograph. The women walking their dog are in Oxgangs Road North which can be seen continuing uphill past the group of trees known as the Cockit Hat. Oxgangs farmhouse is now occupied as Oxgangs Police Station. The name Oxgangs can be traced to the fifteenth century, the *oxgang* being the area of land which could be ploughed by one ox, usually in a team of eight. The houses of Colinton Mains had not yet been built when this photograph was taken. *Courtesy of Allison Naismith and Ian Mitchell.*

Above. The house with the pitched roofs on the left was built in association with Colinton Mains Hospital, better known as the City Hospital. Haystacks at Colinton Mains farm can be seen in front of the houses of Colinton Mains which were built from 1937. *Courtesy of Charles Smith's family.*

[A]

[D]

[B]

[E]

[C]

❧ [A] Strathairly, No. 22 Braidburn Terrace, possibly by John Michael Brown, the artist, who had the house built in 1903.

❧ [B] Swanston Cottage, *c.* 1908, by John Blair (1850–1934).

❧ [C] 'Cottage at Buckstone', probably by Helen P. Thomson who lived at No. 45 Pentland Terrace.

❧ [D] Braid Burn Dairy, Braid Road, by Robert Diaz, on 2 January 1888.

❧ [E] Looking north on Oxgangs Road North near the junction with Redford Road and the Cockit Hat, by Mrs B. Robertson.
All Malcolm Cant Collection.

[A]

[B]

[C]

[D]

[A], [B] and [C] The three images come from the front covers of the sales brochures issued by James Miller & Partners Ltd, the house builders. In the 1930s, prospective purchasers were invited to return a post card, whereupon Miller arranged to send a car for them to visit the various sites. *Courtesy of Mrs Pauline McNaught and Mrs Maria McCallum.*

[D] A similar sales brochure was issued by Hepburn Brothers, the house builders, who claimed that in buying one of their houses: 'there is peace, healthfulness and renewed energy due to the absence of gloom and monotony'. *Malcolm Cant Collection.*

Liberton House, on the south side of Liberton Drive, dates from the late sixteenth century. Following serious fire and water damage in 1991, it was restored by Nicholas Groves-Raines in association with Historic Scotland.
Courtesy of Nicholas Groves-Raines.

[A] Liberton Kirk, designed by the architect, James Gillespie Graham, was built in 1815 on the site of a much older church which had fallen into disrepair.

[B] Liberton Tower, on the north side of Liberton Drive, dates from the fifteenth century. After a long period of neglect, the tower was restored in 1997 by the architects, Simpson & Brown.

[C] The Liberton Inn, in Kirkgate, was originally the village school. The section on the left was the house of Reuben Butler, immortalised as the schoolmaster in Sir Walter Scott's novel, *The Heart of Midlothian*.

[D] The thatched cottages at Swanston had fallen into serious disrepair in the 1950s but were renovated by Edinburgh Corporation. At the present day they are in immaculate condition.

OPPOSITE PAGE
[E] The Royal Observatory on Blackford Hill was opened in 1896 to replace the old Calton Hill Observatory which had fallen into disrepair. The east and west green copper towers have become a distinctive part of the Edinburgh skyline.

[F] Mortonhall House in Frogston Road East was built in 1769 for the Trotter family but is now divided into separate dwellings.

[G] The Nether Liberton doocot, dating from at least the sixteenth century, is one of the biggest in Edinburgh with more than 2,000 nesting boxes.
All photographs by Phil Seale.

❧ [A] Blackford Hill and the Royal Observatory are both dwarfed by the bulk of Arthur's Seat with Sampson's Ribs in the centre of the photograph.

❧ [B] The grand mansion of Hermitage of Braid was built in 1785 for Charles Gordon of Cluny. The property was later acquired by John McDougal who gifted it, and the grounds, to the city in 1938.

❧ [C] From Blackford Hill the view eastwards is to East and West Craiglockhart Hill where all the main buildings are now part of Napier University.

❧ [D] The revolving domes of the Royal Observatory were built by Sir Howard Grubb of Dublin. The telescope in the east dome (seen here) was supplied by Grubb Parsons of Newcastle.

❧ [E] A quiet corner of Blackford Pond which was acquired for the city in 1906. *All photographs by Phil Seale.*

OPPOSITE PAGE

❧ [F] One man with his dog admires the panoramic view north-eastwards from Blackford Hill. The houses nearest to the camera are in Charterhall Road and Grove.

❧ [G] Looking eastwards from the summit of Blackford Hill to Corbie's Crag or Craig, and on to Liberton.

❧ [H] This is no ordinary photograph of general road maintenance. The men are relaying the Hangin' Stanes in Braid Road which mark the spot where the last two highwaymen were executed in Scotland on 25 January 1815. *Photographs [F] and [G] by Phil Seale. Photograph [H] by W. R. Smith.*

❧ [A] Claire Gould, aged 6, of Pentland Primary School, lends support to the ancient Caiy Stane which is believed to be more than 5,000 years old. *Photograph by Douglas A. Gould.*

❧ [B] Face-painting and other attractions in Braidburn Valley Park at the first Fun-Day organised by the Friends of Braidburn Valley Park on 6 September 2003. *Photograph by Lindsay Walls.*

❧ [C] On 13 October 2002 four of the Girl Guides who had assisted with the planting of the cherry trees in 1935 (see page 73), returned, with others, to Braidburn Valley Park to lend their experience to the much lighter task of bulb-planting. *Photograph by Lindsay Walls.*

PART 3

GREENBANK

RISELAW

BRAIDBURN

HERMITAGE

COMISTON

GLENLOCKHART

Part 3, with nearly 70 illustrations, covers much of the area which was previously Greenbank Farm, that is, the present districts of Greenbank and Riselaw. Some idea of what the district looked like 80 years ago can be seen from the photograph on this page. Also included in Part 3 are the surrounding areas of Hermitage Drive, Braid Road and Morningside Drive, as well as South Morningside School, the former City Hospital and Greenlee Old People's Home, and the present Merchants of Edinburgh Golf Club.

The opening section is on Greenbank Farm and the people who worked on the land. Foremost among these are Mr & Mrs Moggie who worked there for nearly 30 years until their way of life was overtaken by urban development. The aerial photograph on page 69 shows just how vulnerable the farmhouse and the steadings were as houses were built further and further up Greenbank Crescent. It is particularly interesting to compare the rural views on page 71 with the present-day layout of Braidburn Valley Park. The construction

of the Open Air Theatre in 1937 completed the transition from farmland to public park.

Around the same time, various firms of builders, from Edinburgh and beyond, were beginning to make their mark on the district. The four main builders were Hepburn, Irvine, Keppie and Robinson, photographs of whom have survived in various family albums. Only a few photographs have been traced of the houses in the course of construction, and none actually showing either the men at work, or the vast quantities of materials being delivered. There is, however, a photograph of unfinished houses in Greenbank Loan immediately adjacent to the roofless Greenbank farmhouse which is obviously about to be demolished. Hepburn's sales brochure has contributed a few ideas on how the houses were furnished, and there are several pictures of residents, either shortly after they moved in, or in the period up to the Second World War. A wartime photograph in Greenbank Crescent shows the owner sitting in his garden with the windows sand-bagged against enemy action.

This photograph, probably taken in the late 1920s from the upper level of Pentland Terrace, gives a panoramic view of Comiston Farm (to the left) and Greenbank Farm, with the trees of the Cockit Hat (at the east end of Redford Road) in the background. *Courtesy of Ian Mitchell.*

❧ The comparable view, taken from about the same position, in 2007, shows that Greenbank Farm is now occupied by Braidburn Valley Park and the houses of Greenbank. *Photograph by Phil Seale.*

shown with a few horse-drawn vehicles but they are obviously not a threat to groups of adults and children having their photograph taken in the middle of the street.

The south corner of Braid Road and Comiston Terrace has been transformed from Hunter's Garage to flatted dwellings, built in 1998. Prior to Hunter's Garage, the corner site was home to the 'tin kirk' built in 1896 as an offshoot of Christ Church Episcopal at Holy Corner. Photographs of the interior of the old church, and of the architect's drawing of it, appear on page 52.

The last few pages of Part 3 are devoted to the City Hospital, the Edinburgh Poorhouse and the Merchants of Edinburgh Golf Club. The City Hospital has been closed for several years but most of the red sandstone buildings have been beautifully restored as private housing. The aerial view which includes the old Poorhouse building gives an excellent overall view and will be of interest to people who now live in the various 'hospital' buildings or the additional houses built in the grounds. The selection concludes with photographs from the archives of the Merchants of Edinburgh Golf Club which has its centenary this year.

The district of Riselaw was also part of Greenbank Farm which extended as far east as Braid Road. Pentland Terrace was built in several sections from 1897 up until the outbreak of the First World War, but many of the houses in the side streets were not built until the 1920s. There are, however, some interesting street scenes, particularly those which show the transition of public transport from cable cars to electric trams, and then to buses.

The 'Braidburn Triangle', bounded by Braidburn Terrace, Braid Road and Pentland Terrace, has been a prolific source of material over the years from Greenbank Parish Church,

Mortonhall Tennis Club (and the curling club before that), and Braidburn Dairy. There are photographs of: the first Greenbank Church; the second one under construction; Curling Pond Cottage; and the quaint corner which was once Braidburn, or Duff's Dairy. A delightful painting of the house, known as Strathairly, in Braidburn Terrace, is reproduced in the colour section.

There are a few pages covering the areas to the east and north of Greenbank Parish Church. The images of Braidburn Terrace, Hermitage Drive and Corrennie Gardens, all taken before 1920, show the streets without any parked vehicles or even passing traffic. Morningside Drive is

❧ Daniel Moggie was born in 1868 at Crichton, Midlothian and married Janet Adam of Tranent at Humbie on 8 October 1889. When they came to Greenbank Farm at the end of the nineteenth century, Daniel worked, firstly, as a ploughman and then as the farm grieve. They had ten children who attended South Morningside School and St Matthew's Parish Church (now Morningside). Mr Moggie's wage was sixteen shillings (80p) per week, plus a tied house and twelve bags of potatoes and twelve bags of turnips per year. In 1926 Daniel and Janet Moggie retired and moved to Millar Crescent. *Courtesy of Bobby Moyes.*

Greenbank Farm and steadings from the air in the early 1930s. Several houses have been built on the east side of Greenbank Crescent but only two blocks on the west side, adjacent to the farmhouse. Part of the old City Poorhouse, now the Steils, shows at the bottom of the picture. The right of way, running obliquely from the hay stacks towards the Poorhouse, is the original Ashy Path. *Courtesy of Edinburgh City Archivist and Malcolm Cant Collection.*

Right. Stooks of corn lie in the field between the Braid Burn and Pentland Terrace. The Braid Hills Hotel, on the higher level, was designed by W. Hamilton Beattie in 1886 but there is doubt about when it actually opened. An early, undated brochure, mentions that 'cable tramways are about to be built', and it is known that the route from Morningside Station was authorised in 1897 and was under trial in 1899. One of the hotel's early attractions was the proximity of the golf courses on the Braid Hills. Appropriately, the hotel has two stained-glass windows depicting golf scenes. *Photograph by R. A. Rayner. Courtesy of Alastair White.*

Below. Daniel and Janet Moggie outside their cottage on Greenbank Farm where they brought up ten children: (listed youngest first) Daniel, Robina, Isabella, Matilda, Marion, John, Elizabeth, Janet, Agnes and Margaret. Their brick-built, slated cottage can be seen in the aerial photograph on page 69 beside the bend in the road before it leads on to Ashy Path. *Courtesy of Dan Moggie.*

Below right. The thatched Greenbank Cottage stood in what is now the back garden ground of Nos 17 & 19 Greenbank Crescent until *c.* 1910 when it was demolished for the construction of Greenbank Crescent. One half of the cottage was the home of the local midwife. *Malcolm Cant Collection.*

Left. The couple in the centre of the picture are strolling in what would, nowadays, be the south end of Fly Walk where it reduces in height as it nears the Braid Burn. It is interesting to note that the right of way is fenced on both sides, presumably to protect the crops. Pentland Terrace can be seen in the background: the high-level section was built in 1897; the section between Braid Hills Road and Riselaw Road was designed in 1903; and the section between Riselaw Road and Place was designed in 1909. It looks as though the spoil from digging the foundations has been dumped on the farm-side of Pentland Terrace.

Below. These two scenes depict, probably more than any other surviving photographs, the rural nature of Greenbank Farm before it succumbed to urban development. On the left, the view is northwards towards the bottom of Greenbank Crescent; on the right, the view is southwards with the hedgerows of Fly Walk on the right. *All photographs by R. A. Rayner. Courtesy of Alastair White.*

❧ *Right.* The ladies of Greenbank Parish Church Women's Guild gather for a group photograph in Braidburn Valley Park in the late 1930s. *Courtesy of Sheila Logie whose mother is on the extreme left of the picture.*

❧ *Below right.* The open-air theatre in Braidburn Valley Park was opened in time for the 1937 Coronation celebrations for King George VI when 1,000 school children gave a massed display of dancing and gymnastics. At the end of the Second World War the theatre was again used by several drama and opera groups including the Southern Light Opera Company, who performed *Merrie England* during the first week of June 1946. The City Parks Department entered into the spirit of the occasion by providing shrubs and flowers for the stage and damming the Braid Burn to provide a sufficient depth of water for Queen Elizabeth to make her triumphal entry by Royal Barge. *Courtesy of the family of the late Mrs G. Lowson.*

❧ *Below.* Queen Elizabeth (Mrs G. Lowson) in the Southern Light Opera Company's production of *Merrie England*. *Courtesy of the family of the late Mrs G. Lowson.*

✤ *Above*. Daniel Moggie at his allotment in Braidburn Valley Park in 1944. The allotments were part of the 'Dig for Victory' campaign at the beginning of the Second World War, but were still in use in the 1960s. Daniel probably knew the condition of the soil better than many of his fellow allotment holders as he had been a ploughman and then the grieve at Greenbank until his retirement in 1926. *Courtesy of Dan Moggie.*

✤ *Above left*. This view, looking south from Braidburn Valley Park, is undated but cannot be earlier than the late 1930s. The land has obviously been laid out as a public park, the cherry trees planted by the youth organisations in 1935 are evident on the left, and the telegraph poles have been erected for the houses in Greenbank Crescent. *Courtesy of Louise Jenkins.*

✤ *Left*. Taken by the same photographer, Sutherland, this view shows the open-air theatre, the houses of Greenbank Crescent, and a few, newly built houses in Pentland Gardens. *Courtesy of Alex Segger.*

Both photographs are of Theodore K. Irvine: on the left Mr Irvine is formally dressed in the robes of Provost of Bathgate; and, on the right, he appears as a much younger man in Highland dress. Theodore K. Irvine, a native of Lerwick, came to Edinburgh as a young man where he qualified as an architect and set up in business as a builder and architect. He later moved to Bathgate where he was Provost from 1937 until his premature death in 1939. At Greenbank in the 1930s he designed and built Nos 20–30 (even), the Crescent, and in the Road, Nos 21–33 (odd) and Nos 8–26 (even), but excluding No. 20 which was built by Ford & Torrie of Queen Street for the Napier family. *Courtesy of West Lothian Council Libraries.*

❧ *Above left.* Bowlers, cigars, waistcoats and walking sticks are all part of the uniform of this group of young men photographed at Dunfermline in the early part of the twentieth century. The man on the left is James Hepburn, and the man in the centre (front) is Lawrence Hepburn, both of Hepburn Brothers, the builders. The identity of the others is not known. Hepburn built many more houses in Greenbank than any of the other builders. *Courtesy of Mrs Sheila Hepburn.*

❧ *Above centre.* Three generations – all Simon Keppie – at Yewlands Gardens, Liberton, *c.* 1930. The two men were father and son in the building firm of Simon Keppie & Son. The third Simon Keppie was a pupil at the Royal High School when the photograph was taken: later in life he qualified as an actuary and became an Assistant General Manager with the Standard Life Assurance Company of Edinburgh. At Greenbank, Simon Keppie built Nos 2–8 (even), the Loan, and Nos 32–54 (even), the Crescent. *Courtesy of J. C. Keppie.*

❧ *Above right.* William Robinson, eldest son of Richard Robinson the builder (and brother of Richard J. Robinson) on the day of his marriage to Agnes Angus on 16 September 1927. *Courtesy of the Robinson family.*

❧ *Right.* Richard J. Robinson worked with his father, also Richard, in the construction of houses in Greenbank Drive, Lane, Loan and Road in the 1930s. He is photographed here in 1927 when he was best man at the wedding of his brother, William. *Courtesy of the Robinson family.*

Above. Nos 11 & 13 Greenbank Row have just been completed by Hepburn Brothers, and the front gardens have been laid out. The remainder of the north side of the Row, and the entire south side have not yet been built. The photograph was taken from the driveway of No. 9 in 1934. No. 11 was constructed from a very hard red brick known as Accrington Nori at the request of the first owner, David Watson, a marine engineer, who had spent many years working in London. The special construction added £75 to the cost of the house. *Courtesy of the Watson family.*

Above right. The house under construction by Robinson the builder, on the right of the picture, is No. 5 Greenbank Loan, and the house on the left is No. 52 Greenbank Crescent by Simon Keppie & Son. Between the two is the roofless shell of Greenbank farmhouse, *c.* 1934. When the land was being feued for building purposes there was a proposal to renovate the old farmhouse and retain it in the new district, but, unfortunately the idea was abandoned. *Courtesy of the McIlwrick family.*

Right. This photograph of Greenbank Loan was taken, *c.* 1935, from the upper windows of No. 50 Greenbank Crescent which, at the time, was owned by Thomas Robert McIlwrick. On the left-hand side there is a board in the front garden saying 'Robinson's Bungalows', and a few houses further on, on the right, there is another sign which was probably for the show house. *Courtesy of the McIlwrick family.*

❧ *Left.* Hepburn Brothers took great pride in their sales literature and issued several brochures with photographs of house interiors including this one furnished by J. & R. Allan. Hepburn also liked to point out that there was money, time and effort to be saved by moving to one of their modern bungalows: 'Gas and electricity in the modern house is equivalent to the saving of a maid, or alternatively, the saving of drudgery to the housewife.'

❧ *Below left.* In 1932 a Hepburn bungalow cost between £560 and £950. The cheapest house, at £560, was a semi-detached three-roomed bungalow with kitchen and bathroom, and £585 if detached. At the top end of the market was Hepburn's 6-apartment 'cottage' with a very desirable specification which included four clothes poles, fencing, double gates, four open fires, a 'Ready to Work' kitchenette and all walls papered at two shillings (10p) per roll.

❧ *Below.* Hepburn was not averse to highlighting what they saw as the disadvantages of other sectors of the housing market: 'The largest of our residences are all specifically designed and arranged to replace the depressing Victorian house with its damp, dark cellars, long corridors and windowless staircase.' This couple would have paid less than £5 every four weeks over a period of 25 years for a 90% loan on a £950 Hepburn house.
All Malcolm Cant Collection

❧ *Right.* This photograph was taken in 1936 in the back garden of No. 11 Greenbank Row. When Bob Watson was diagnosed with osteomyelitis, part of the recommended treatment was to sleep in the open air. A few years later, in 1939, at the outbreak of the Second World War, he was obliged to abandon the idea as it was thought that the presence of a tent, and possibly a light at night, would attract the attention of enemy aircraft. *Courtesy of the Watson family.*

❧ *Below.* Margaret Tullis and her aunt, also Margaret Tullis, in the fields at the back of No. 55 Greenbank Road, *c.* 1933. The house was built by Robinson, the builder, and bought by James Tullis, the decorator, shortly before the photograph was taken. *Courtesy of the Tullis family.*

❧ *Below right.* Betty Comrie, on the left, and Sheila Logie, on the right, outside No. 71 Greenbank Road, *c.* 1937. Betty lived at No. 73 with her parents who ran the nursery at Holy Corner, and Sheila lived at No. 71. The house name, Com-Bo-Craig, was taken from various Edinburgh place names associated with the family. *Courtesy of Sheila Logie.*

❧ *Left.* Robert White (1873–1953), the founding principal of Robert White & Co. SSC, of No. 32 Queen Street, Edinburgh, lived at No. 31 Greenbank Crescent for many years. He is seen here visiting the home of his friend, Thomas R. McIlwrick, of No. 50 Greenbank Crescent. *Courtesy of the McIlwrick family.*

❧ *Right.* James 'Ian' Stewart of Stewart & Co., Seedsmen, No. 13 South St Andrew Street and his second daughter, Moyra, at No. 122 Greenbank Crescent in 1940. The window is protected against enemy action by a timber frame loaded with sandbags and covered by a mesh tarpaulin. *Courtesy of Mrs Sheila Bulmer, née Stewart.*

Right. Margaret Glegg is on the left with Alan Little and his mother, Nellie Little, at No. 11 Pentland Terrace in 1934. Alan Little emigrated to the United States and worked for the Kennedy administration. Margaret Glegg was the daughter of William Daniel Glegg co-founder of the iron and steel merchants, Brown & Glegg, who had their offices at No. 38 Candlemaker Row. *Courtesy of Graham Moonie.*

Below right. A young family group on Comiston Road in 1911 near to the flight of steps which leads to the high-level section of Pentland Terrace. On the right of the picture, a cable car is waiting at the Braid Hills terminus. *Malcolm Cant Collection.*

Below. Most of this young group appear reluctant to face the camera or perhaps they have been asked by the photographer to adopt a casual demeanour. The undated photograph was taken at the corner of Pentland Terrace and Braid Hills Road. *Malcolm Cant Collection.*

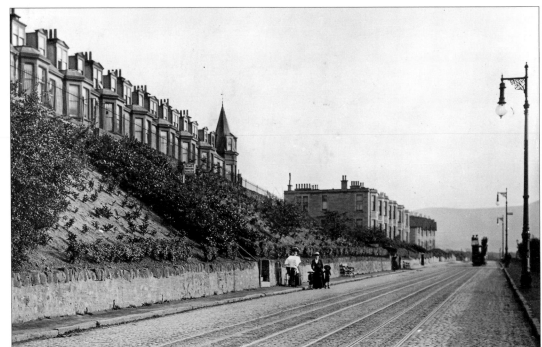

❧ *Left.* When the Braid Hills Hotel was opened in the 1890s, it had a very clear view of the city as the bungalows of Greenbank and Riselaw had not yet been built. The glasshouse, seen in the picture, was in use until 1986 when it was demolished for the construction of the new dining room. *Malcolm Cant Collection.*

❧ *Below left.* A lot of stone setts have been lifted around the track at the Braid Hills tram terminus which was not extended to Fairmilehead until 19 April 1936. The tram has been converted from a cable car and has the upper deck only partially enclosed. *Courtesy of A. W. Brotchie.*

❧ *Below.* The undated photograph was taken at the junction of Riselaw Road and Pentland Terrace. The terraced houses on the north side of Riselaw Road were designed by Lyle & Constable and built by W. G. Davies. On the right, No. 20 Pentland Terrace was part of the 1909 terrace, built by John C. White. *Malcolm Cant Collection.*

Right. Standard electric tram 211 on service No. 11 on Pentland Terrace between Braid Hills Road and Riselaw Road, on 30 January 1954. The service was converted from the old cable car system on 18 March 1923. *Courtesy of George Fairley.*

Below. On 18 September 1954 the junction of Comiston Road, Greenbank Crescent and Braidburn Terrace had no need of traffic lights. To the left of the tram car, two people are waiting at the stop which is marked by a small sign on the overhead wire support pole, 'CARS TO TOWN STOP HERE'. On the right, the new bus stop will be in use the following day as the buses take over. The tram stop sign on the up line can just be seen on the support pole partly into Braidburn Terrace. *Courtesy of George Fairley.*

Below right. Almost 53 years later, the location is still obvious but the bus stops have been moved away from the busy junction controlled by traffic lights. *Photograph by Phil Seale.*

☙ *Above left.* Greenbank United Presbyterian Church was opened on 13 May 1900 in what is now the eastmost hall of Greenbank Parish Church. In the same year the name was changed to Greenbank United Free Church at the union of the United Presbyterian Church and the Free Church. The second church, built to the west, was dedicated on 8 October 1927. The photograph shows the assembled company present at the laying of the foundation stone on 24 April 1926.
Photograph by George Blyth Logie.
Courtesy of Greenbank Parish Church.

☙ *Above.* The huge reinforced concrete beams of the nave are slowly being surrounded by the supporting masonry of Greenbank United Free Church. On the right is the foundation stone in the wall, and the builder's board 'Wm. Gerard & Sons, Main Contractor'. The church took its present name, Greenbank Parish Church, in 1929, at the historic union of the Church of Scotland. *Courtesy of Greenbank Parish Church.*

☙ *Left.* Some of the enthusiastic volunteers outside Greenbank Parish Church hall who helped to collect this huge consignment of clothing for Hungary at the time of the uprising in 1956.
Courtesy of Greenbank Parish Church.

❧ *Right.* The cows are grazing in a field now occupied by the terraced houses on the south side of Braidburn Terrace. The large buttressed building is the first Greenbank Church, and the small building on the left is Curling Pond Cottage.
Courtesy of Greenbank Parish Church.

❧ *Below right.* This picture of Greenbank United Presbyterian Church was taken from Braid Road, showing, on the right, the terraced houses on the north side of Braidburn Terrace. Mortonhall Curling Club pond is in the foreground, which was probably in use between about 1890 and 1914. *Courtesy of Greenbank Parish Church.*

❧ *Below.* This elegantly dressed 1913 group, at the site of Mortonhall Tennis Club, is a bit of an enigma. There is no doubt about the date of the photograph but the club's records show that the original feu charter for the club's use of the ground was registered on 21 May 1926. *Malcolm Cant Collection.*

Left. Many photographs survive of Braidburn Dairy, or Duff's Dairy, which lay in the narrow gusset of land on the west side of Braid Road, almost opposite the entrance to the Hermitage of Braid. The entry for Braidburn Dairy in the 1891 Census included William Mitchell, his wife Grace and their two daughters and one son, along with Mary Sterrat, the dairymaid, and Robert Jackson, a farm servant. *Malcolm Cant Collection.*

Below. This late nineteenth-century view of Braidburn Dairy was taken from the position of the present day tennis courts at Mortonhall. The stone bridge over the Braid Burn can just be seen on the extreme right of the picture. This is where David Loch, a carter from Biggar, was attacked by Thomas Kelly and Henry Orneil on 23 November 1814. At their subsequent trial before the Lord Justice Clerk the two men were found guilty and sentenced to be hanged, in the words of the judge 'not at the ordinary place but on the spot where you robbed and assaulted David Loch, or as near as possible to that spot'. The Hanging Stanes were erected further north opposite No. 66 Braid Road. See also page 63. *Courtesy of Greenbank Parish Church.*

Below left. Curling Pond Cottage, or Braidburn Cottage, occupied a very idyllic spot. The building was used from around 1890 in connection with Mortonhall Curling Club and then by Mortonhall Tennis Club until it was demolished in 1957. The upper storey was also used as a private house at various times. *Malcolm Cant Collection.*

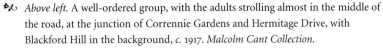

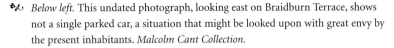

❧ *Above left.* A well-ordered group, with the adults strolling almost in the middle of the road, at the junction of Corrennie Gardens and Hermitage Drive, with Blackford Hill in the background, *c.* 1917. *Malcolm Cant Collection.*

❧ *Below left.* This undated photograph, looking east on Braidburn Terrace, shows not a single parked car, a situation that might be looked upon with great envy by the present inhabitants. *Malcolm Cant Collection.*

❧ *Above right.* A few years earlier, *c.* 1911, a similar scene, devoid of vehicular traffic, at the junction of Hermitage Gardens and Hermitage Drive. *Malcolm Cant Collection.*

❧ *Below right.* Braidburn Terrace at a relatively quiet time of day in 2007. Prior to 1905 the street was named Greenbank Road, taking its name from the narrow track which led to Greenbank Farm. *Photograph by Phil Seale.*

✤ *Left.* Hunter's Garage in Braid Road was built in 1922 on the site of the derelict 'tin kirk', built in 1896 for Christ Church at Holy Corner. The photograph shows several Morgan cars at the garage in 1988. The business was established in 1919 in two modest huts in a pend off Balcarres Street by William Hay Hunter who opened the Braid Road premises in 1922. Bill Hunter joined his father in the business in 1946, and by the 1950s there were plans for expansion. Unfortunately, planning permission was not granted for an ambitious scheme to build a new two-storey garage, with access from Braid Road and Comiston Road, on ground to the south of Mortonhall Tennis Club. However, Braidburn Service Station was opened in 1962 and continued until 1990 when the Gulf Service Station (later Shell) was built. *Courtesy of Bill Hunter.*

✤ *Below left.* In 1997 the main garage in Braid Road was closed bringing to an end nearly 80 years of service by three generations of the Hunter family, Bill Hunter's son, Alistair, having joined the firm in 1984. By 1998, when this photograph was taken, the girder work for flatted dwellings was well advanced. *Malcolm Cant Collection.*

✤ *Below.* The flats which now occupy the site are visually pleasing and compatible with the surrounding architecture. *Photograph by Phil Seale.*

Right. This undated photograph shows Greenbank Terrace, looking north to Morningside Station. Most of the right-hand side of the road is under repair where the setts have been lifted from around the cable car tracks. Greenbank Terrace was built in two separate phases: the east side (right) was constructed by James Slater, the builder, of No. 71 Albert Street and was occupied from 1886; the west side (left) was built much later by William McNiven & Sons who obtained permission to build in 1906. *Courtesy of Peter Sutherland.*

Below. In 1987 the East Lodge for the Craiglockhart Poorhouse was completely derelict and was demolished shortly thereafter for the construction of Greenbank House. The lodge was No. 144 Comiston Road which was the address used on birth certificates and death certificates in an effort to remove the perceived stigma of having been born, or having died, in the Poorhouse. The photograph shows the pedestrian entrance and the pillars to the driveway which ran parallel to Greenbank Drive. *Malcolm Cant Collection.*

Below right. When this photograph of South Morningside School was taken from Braid Crescent, the playground was divided by a railing, with the girls on the south side and the boys on the north. Boys and girls entered by separate doors and even in the classrooms the girls sat at one side and the boys at the other. Pupils were first admitted on 5 September 1892, 80% of whom were from addresses north of Morningside Station. The school was formally opened by Andrew Carnegie on 3 October 1892 and has continued its high standard of education ever since.
Courtesy of Charles J. Smith's family.

Above. A very mixed group of children and adults pose for the camera in this 1905 picture taken at the top of Morningside Drive near the junction with St Clair Terrace. One of the men looks as though he is wearing a railway uniform and the boy on the extreme right is carrying a milk pitcher. *Malcolm Cant Collection.*

Left. A series of photographs was taken by John Patrick within a few moments of one another probably from one of the upper windows in Comiston Road. At the time, James Patrick, the photographer, lived at No. 63 Comiston Road, and John Patrick, also a photographer, lived at No. 52. In the top left-hand corner of the photograph there is a 'To Let' sign outside the top flat window for 'E. Calvert 16 N. St. And. St.'. Edward Calvert was a well-known architect and surveyor who had his offices in North St Andrew Street in the early 1900s.
Malcolm Cant Collection.

Right. Colinton Mains Hospital, or the City Hospital as it came to be known, was opened on 13 May 1903 by King Edward VII in the presence of the Lord Provost, James Steel, and numerous civic dignitaries. Immediately after the opening ceremony, King Edward conferred a baronetcy on Lord Provost Steel. The opening was a very grand affair with a processional route through Morningside, up Comiston Road and along what is now Greenbank Drive. *Malcolm Cant Collection.*

Below right. This early photograph shows that the City Hospital was built on a green-field site, away from any urban development. It was the brain-child of both Bailie James Pollard, Convener of the City's Public Health Committee, and Edinburgh's first Medical Officer of Health, Dr Henry Littlejohn (knighted in 1895) whose *Report on the Sanitary Condition of the City of Edinburgh* in 1865 said that 'Disease is spreading like wildfire in houses without proper running water and flush toilets'. The Town Council responded with piecemeal initiatives but it was not until a serious outbreak of smallpox in 1894 that any real progress was made for a new fever hospital. Colinton Mains Farm was bought for £20,500, the City Architect, Robert Morham, was instructed to draw up plans, and the first turf was cut in May 1897 by Lady McDonald. *Malcolm Cant Collection.*

Below. A plethora of signs at the entrance to the City Hospital in 1998 as it awaits closure. The definitive history of the hospital *The Edinburgh City Hospital* was written by Dr James A. Gray, Consultant Physician in Communicable Diseases in the Regional Infectious Diseases Unit between 1969 and 1995, and published in 1999. *Photograph by Phyllis M. Cant.*

This aerial photograph of the City Hospital, *c.* 1931, provides an excellent view of the overall layout which provided plenty of space for the control of infectious diseases. The buildings in the bottom left-hand corner of the photograph were the wards for the isolation of smallpox. The City Poorhouse, later used as Greenlea Old People's Home, can be seen on the left. In recent years, both the City Hospital and Greenlea have been redeveloped for private housing. *Courtesy of Edinburgh City Archivist and Malcolm Cant Collection.*

❧ *Above right.* The Merchants of Edinburgh Golf Club was established on Easter and Wester Craiglockhart Hill on 6 November 1907 when a group of 'merchants, clergymen, doctors, lawyers, journalists and others' decided to form a club. The photograph shows the members of the Provisional and Club Councils for 1907, 1908 and 1909. *Back row*: T. R. McIlwrick; D. Thompson; James Waugh; John Mackenzie. *Middle row*: John Milne; J. Scott Marshall; W. A. Middleton; P. Waldie; Allan McGill; J. C. H. Balmain; William Alston. *Seated*: D. Reid; W. Bryden Hogg; William Lindsay; John Gibson; James Summers. *Reclining*: Alfred J. F. Mitchell. The present Club is in the process of producing the centenary history which will be published in 2008.

❧ *Above.* During the winter of 1982, when the Merchants of Edinburgh Golf Course was in the grip of a mini ice-age, the members turned their allegiance, temporarily, to the game of curling.

❧ *Right.* Two players holing out on the 18th green unruffled by the impending cut. The photograph is undated but must be before 8 February 1959, being the date when the No. 39 bus service was diverted from Greenbank Row to Greenbank Drive. In the photograph, the double-decker bus is negotiating Greenbank Lane without difficulty, unimpeded by parked cars. *All courtesy of the Merchants of Edinburgh Golf Club.*

PART 4

BLACKFORD HILL

HERMITAGE OF BRAID

BRAID HILLS

Part 4, dealing with Blackford Hill, the Hermitage of Braid and the Braid Hills, is the shortest of the four sections, but, nevertheless, contains over 40 interesting photographs. In this Introduction there are three unusual views: one of Mortonhall Golf Clubhouse taken from the Braid Hills; another of the old road to Liberton; and a panoramic view of the Grange and Newington districts taken from Blackford Hill. In each case there are wide open spaces where roads and houses now stand.

The section continues with views of the main access points to Blackford Hill, namely the entrance at Charterhall Road and the much steeper approach through the Harrison Arch and up Observatory Road. This is where Imshi the donkey comes into her own. To the east, on the long sloping tail of Blackford Hill, two very different enterprises were established. Craigmillar Park Golf Club came there in 1906, having been first established at Crawfurd Road in 1895. The much less peaceful operation was

Blackford Quarry which ceased operations in the 1950s following a public enquiry to look into its proposed extension. The photograph of the quarrymen in 1928 shows that there was a fairly substantial workforce.

There are several pictures of Blackford Pond taken from different angles and at different times of year, the most interesting, perhaps, being the winter scenes when the ice was sufficiently weight-bearing to allow skating. It is also interesting to note how the position of the

❧ The narrow road, with the dry-stane dykes on each side, was the forerunner to Braid Hills Drive. It cut through the golf courses on Braid Hills, a few hundred yards south of the present road alignment. The small loch, or skating pond, with the picturesque island was drained (much to the relief of the golfers) and the road realigned in the mid-1920s. *Photograph by R. A. Rayner. Courtesy of Alastair White.*

❧ Mortonhall Golf Clubhouse photographed from the Braid Hills with the Pentland Hills in the background. The club was established in 1892 and the clubhouse, designed by Sydney Mitchell, was opened on 11 February 1893. *Photograph by R. A. Rayner. Courtesy of Alastair White.*

❧ The photograph taken from Blackford Hill shows that not all of the Grange and Newington had been built up. Much of West Savile Terrace is not completed and there is a lot of undeveloped ground to the north of the suburban railway line. *Malcolm Cant Collection.*

various pathways and the extent of the vegetation have altered over the years.

Within a stone's throw of Blackford Pond is the Braid Estate Recreation Ground, established in 1890, home of the Braid Tennis Club and the Braid Bowling Club. Among the various club photographs is one of the 'Canadian Tour, 1913' in which the bowling clubhouse is bedecked with flags.

A few of the attractive walks on Blackford Hill are also included from the notable Yerbury

Collection of Edinburgh material. The first shows people of various ages walking on the path beside Corbie's Crag, and, the second, a group of, as yet, unidentified photographers resting near Blackford Quarry. Hermitage of Braid, which now has a visitors' centre, is also to be found.

By far the most dominant building on Blackford Hill is the Royal Observatory opened in 1896 to replace the observatory on Calton Hill. A great many people know the building from the outside but not so many have seen inside the

distinctive green copper towers or the large modern structures in which instruments are designed and assembled for use in outer space.

There are also golfing scenes on the Braid Hills including an early photograph of lady golfers driving off from the tee beside Winchester's Refreshment Rooms.

The final page is of Braid Farm, which lay between the Braid Hills and the Hermitage of Braid.

❧ *Right.* The north entrance to Blackford Hill and Blackford Pond looks very rural compared to the present-day road junction of Cluny Gardens/Charterhall Road and Oswald Road. The photograph clearly shows the semi-circular entrance beside the park-keeper's lodge, but Cluny Gardens (to the right) has not been fully developed at that point. On Blackford Hill, the position of the various pathways appears to have been altered over the years and there is not nearly so much vegetation on the hill as there is nowadays.

❧ *Below.* In this later view of the same location, the garden area of the lodge has matured and a gas-lit lamp standard has been erected beside the gates. Cluny Gardens also has a better road surface and there is a pavement, at least on the south side of the road.

❧ *Below right.* By the time of this early 1920s photograph, the junction has been upgraded to cope with the increase in vehicular traffic. The roadway is properly surfaced, there are pavements and kerb stones. In the bottom left-hand corner, there is the suggestion of double-yellow lines; they are, in fact, granite setts laid parallel to the kerb to form a gutter.
All Malcolm Cant Collection.

BLACKFORD HILL

ENTRANCE TO BLACKFORD HILL, EDINBURGH.

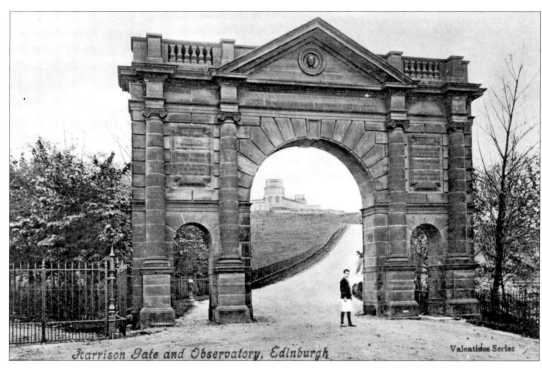

Harrison Gate and Observatory, Edinburgh.   Valentines Series

Harrison Arch, Blackford, Edinburgh.   A.2609.

❧ *Above left.* The Harrison Arch, at the entrance to Observatory Road, was erected to commemorate the efforts of Lord Provost Sir George Harrison in the purchase, in 1884, of Blackford Hill by the City of Edinburgh from the Trotter family for the sum of £8,000. George Harrison entered the Town Council in 1879 and was Lord Provost from 1882 to 1885. *Malcolm Cant Collection.*

❧ *Left.* A more recent picture of Observatory Road shows the bungalows which were built on the south side of the road from the late 1920s. *Malcolm Cant Collection.*

❧ *Above.* The houses in Observatory Road have a magnificent view out over the city but during the Second World War when the use of private vehicles was severely restricted, mothers had a difficult job transporting children and provisions to the top of the hill. The Downes family solved the problem by acquiring a donkey. The photograph shows Jennifer Downes in 1943 on Imshi at the top of Observatory Road, with the family home in the background. Jennifer's father was William Gordon Greensmith Downes of Greensmith Downes, the ladies' fashion shop in Princes Street. *Courtesy of Jenni Pickwell.*

Right. Craigmillar Park Golf Club celebrated its centenary in 1995. When the club history was being researched, it was discovered that the earliest minute books had extremely limited information. However, a report in *The Scotsman* was traced, dated 12 January 1895, which confirmed that: 'A nine-hole golf course was being formed at Craigmillar Park', with its main entrance from Crawfurd Road. A further report in *The Scotsman* confirmed that the club was opened on Saturday 5 October 1895. Within the first decade, however, there were several intimations by the landowners that parts of the course were required for building feus. By 1906 the club had negotiated a new lease with the Trotters of Mortonhall for the present site on Blackford Hill. Play began in October 1906 but the course was not extended to 18 holes until May 1927. In 1961, the club held a two-round handicap open tournament which by 1971 had become a 72-hole scratch tournament for elite amateur golfers. Notable winners include Nick Faldo in 1976, and, more recently, Marc Warren and Lloyd Saltman. The club history, *Craigmillar Park Golf Club 1895–1995*, by William Russell, gives an excellent account of how the club developed from inception. The photograph shows Sir Samuel Chapman playing off at the official opening of the 18-hole course on 14 May 1927. The opening shot is said to have 'gone down West Mains Road via a cottage roof'.

Below. A foursome tees off with considerable style and ability at the tenth hole in 1995.

Below right. The photograph shows the clubhouse as extended in 1937. It was extended again to create a much more modern building in 1970 which, sadly, was extensively damaged by fire in 1979. The present clubhouse was built in the early 1980s and extended in 1996.
All photographs courtesy of Craigmillar Park Golf Club.

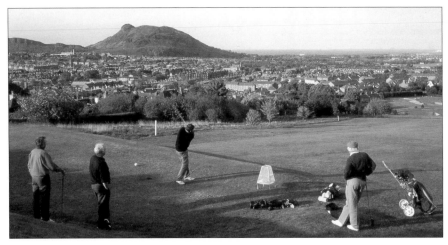

When this photograph was taken in 1928, Blackford Quarry employed a substantial number of men, almost all of whom wore a working man's bunnet and strong boots with reinforced toecaps. Their foreman, Andrew Alexander, is first from the left in the second front row. Andrew was born at Greenends on 19 November 1878 and died on 8 June 1934. His grave in Liberton Kirkyard is marked by the family headstone and an additional stone with the words: 'In memory of Andrew Alexander for 21 years foreman at Blackford Quarry, from the employees, 1934'. Andrew was the father of Margaret (Peggy) Alexander, the Highland dancer, whose photograph appears on page 22. *Courtesy of Mrs Margaret Allan, née Thomson.*

❧ *Above left.* Looking west at Blackford Pond with the smaller pond, fenced off, at the bottom left-hand corner of the picture. The photograph also shows that in the early days there was an access path round the south side of the Pond. *Malcolm Cant Collection.*

❧ *Above right.* This 1923 picture, also looking west, shows the much broader, more sheltered pathway with the south-facing benches. *Malcolm Cant Collection.*

❧ *Below left and right.* The photographs show a popular spot for children and adults with bicycles and prams. Feeding the ducks and swans has been a local tradition ever since the area was acquired for the city in 1906. *Courtesy of Alex Segger.*

❧ *Above left.* Blackford Pond, photographed from the hill, looking towards the houses on Cluny Gardens. The Astley Ainslie Hospital with its open verandas and well-cultivated vegetable beds can be seen in the top right-hand corner. *Malcolm Cant Collection.*

❧ *Above right.* One of Edinburgh's classic views is of Blackford Pond with the houses of the Grange in the middle distance and Arthur's Seat beyond. The photograph has been taken from open ground now occupied as allotments. *Malcolm Cant Collection.*

❧ *Below left and right.* These two views taken by Rayner, the photographer, show how popular the pond was for winter sports. It was the home of the Waverley Curling Club, established in 1848, and there is photographic evidence to show that curling was still being played at Blackford Pond well into the twentieth century. *Photographs by R. A. Rayner. Courtesy of Alastair White.*

❧ *Right.* This photograph, with the original clubhouse in the background, was taken in August 1993 when the Edinburgh Women's Bowling Association held its championship finals day at Braid. The lady in the centre is Mrs Aimee Robertson of Braid Bowling Club who was the President of the EWBA during 1993. *Courtesy of Braid Bowling Club.*

❧ *Below right.* Informal centenary celebrations were held by the tennis club which was also founded in 1890. Seated at the front, from right to left, are: Jenny, Frankie, Mary, David, Kerr, Brian and Norma. Myrra is in the left alcove and Janette, Diane and Ruth are on the right. *Photograph by Lois Bain.*

❧ *Below.* An all-weather surface was installed at the club in April 1980 which greatly extended the playing season. Two volunteers are equipped ready to assist the groundsman: Mrs Val Walker on the left and Miss Lois Bain on the right. *Courtesy of Lois Bain.*

❧ *Opposite page.* This illustration, entitled Canadian Tour 1913, is taken from a framed picture that hangs in the old clubhouse of Braid Bowling Club, established in 1890. On the reverse of the picture, which shows the 1901 clubhouse, only one person is identified, namely 'Andrew Hamilton, second row from back, fourth from right, wearing straw hat'. Andrew Haig Hamilton of Lutton Place Bowling Club was secretary of the Scottish Bowling Association from 1895 until 1936.

When the Gordons of Cluny were feuing out parts of their land to the south of the suburban railway they made provision for recreational space, but the feu charters made each feuar responsible for paying for a share of the ground and its upkeep thereafter. A bowling green, lawn tennis courts and two small pavilions were provided, initially only for the use of the house owners and their families resident with them in a designated area. *Courtesy of Braid Bowling Club.*

Right. A group of well-dressed photographers, *c.* 1900, relaxes at Blackford Glen after logging up a few more hours carrying fairly bulky equipment. Unfortunately, the identity of the photographers has not been established. The photograph appears to have been taken near Blackford Quarry, not far from the Agassiz Rock, an interesting geological feature named after Lois Agassiz, the Swiss geologist. *Yerbury Collection.*

Below right. Children, who have probably been playing in the Braid Burn, pose for the camera on the path which runs from the Hermitage of Braid to Liberton Dams.
Malcolm Cant Collection.

Below. The hill path, between the east end of Hermitage of Braid and Corbie's Crag or Craig, attracted walkers of all ages in the 1880s. The photograph was probably taken shortly after Blackford Hill was opened to the citizens of Edinburgh in 1884. *Yerbury Collection.*

❧ *Above left*. The mansion of Hermitage of Braid was built in 1785 for Charles Gordon of Cluny. The design, probably by Robert Burn, in a romantically defensive style, has mock machicolations, battlements and even pointed, dummy bartizans on the corners. It was Charles Gordon who was responsible for laying out the grounds with lawns and various species of trees. The old walled garden, the lectern-style doocot and the ice-house are extant, but the corn mill to the west of the house has long since been demolished. After the Gordons ceased to live at the Hermitage, their trustees let the property to several tenants, including Sir John Skelton, the advocate. The house and grounds were purchased by John McDougal from the trustees for £11,000 and in 1938 were gifted to the city as a public park. In more recent years, the house has been used as a Scout hostel and is now a visitors' centre and base for the Countryside Ranger Service. *Malcolm Cant Collection.*

❧ *Above*. The Hermitage of Braid in its modern setting is substantially unaltered, externally, from the original design. *Photograph by Phil Seale.*

❧ *Left*. William Wilkie, the farmer, kept some of his working horses in a field adjacent to the Hermitage in the 1920s. Mr Wilkie farmed at Braid Farm nearby and also at Comiston Farm. *Courtesy of Miss Isla Wilkie.*

Right. The Royal Observatory on Blackford Hill was opened in 1896 to replace the Calton Hill Observatory which had fallen into disrepair. As the new observatory was quite remote from the city, the grounds contained houses for the Astronomer Royal and his assistants, stables and even vegetable gardens. In the background of the picture there are no houses on Observatory Road.

Below. This telescope was supplied for use in the East Tower in 1928 by Grubb Parsons of Newcastle. It was used regularly until the 1970s when professional astronomical observing was moved to mountain-top sites, such as Mauna Kea in Hawaii, which has a much drier atmosphere.

Below right. This aerial view shows the East and West Towers with the library block at right angles. The detached building to the left of centre is the Astronomer Royal's house. The light-coloured modern building, erected in 1963 and extended in 1967, was built to contain laboratories for the new discipline of electrical engineering. The building now houses the Institute for Astronomy of the University of Edinburgh. *All photographs courtesy of The Royal Observatory Edinburgh.*

Left. This 1993 aerial view shows many modern developments in addition to the original buildings. In the right-hand corner of the picture are buildings housing machining workshops, laboratories and the canteen. To the west of the site (bottom left) are a block of offices and several small buildings, including two telescope domes, which were all replaced in 2005 by the Crawford Building and Laboratories.

Below left. The original Observatory buildings on Blackford Hill were designed by W. W. Robertson, and built by W. & J. Kirkwood, with the work on the revolving domes being done by Sir Howard Grubb of Dublin. The East and West Towers can be seen on the right, linked by a flat roof which was designed as an observing platform for small instruments. On the left of the picture is the Meridian House which contained a transit circle (an instrument used to measure the position of a star in the sky). The Royal Observatory was also a meteorological station.

Below. This is the interior of the Crawford Laboratory opened in 2005. This spacious facility can accommodate the large instruments that are designed and assembled in Edinburgh and sent to modern telescopes in Hawaii, Chile and even into space. *All photographs courtesy of The Royal Observatory Edinburgh.*

The photograph was taken at the old tenth tee on the Braids where a ladies' match is in progress, watched by a crowd of men and women. The tee was adjacent to what was known as Winchester's Refreshment Rooms which were very popular with the golfing fraternity. The Winchesters appear to have been resident there when it was still a farmhouse, and again when one of the family was the starter on the course. Later, when Stan Smith's family took the tenancy in the 1930s, the house still had no gas, electricity or running water. 'Granny' Smith dispensed lemonade and biscuits to the golfers from the open kitchen window.
Photograph by R. A. Rayner.
Courtesy of Alastair White.

In this 1905 view of the west side of the Braid Hills the adjacent buildings on the left are the Golfers' Rest (nearest to the camera) and the Golfers' Tryst. The Golfers' Tryst was opened by William Frier in 1892 as a clubhouse, tea-room and shop. The Golfers' Rest, built about the same time, was owned by Mrs May Mackay and Lindsay Goldie Ross, who was the first professional to be appointed at the Braids. At the present day the Golfers' Tryst is owned by the Braids Tryst Ltd, and is the home of the Braids United Golf Club and the Edinburgh Western Golf Club. Other clubs based at the Braids include the Harrison Golf Club and the Edinburgh Thistle Golf Club. The other building, in the centre of the picture, built by Edinburgh Corporation in 1897, provided living accommodation for the greenkeeper and the course superintendent at either end, and the professional's shop in the centre. Golf has probably been played informally on the Braids for nearly 400 years. The present-day No. 1 course was opened in 1889 and No. 2 course in 1894, initially as a 9-hole course only.
Malcolm Cant Collection.

❧ *Above left.* Braid farmhouse and steadings lay between Braid Hills Drive and the Hermitage of Braid. The farmhouse is to the right of the stack yard. The other farm buildings include the byre, the barn and a horse gin in which a horse, at one time, was tethered to rotate giant mill stones.
Courtesy of Charles J. Smith's family.

❧ *Above.* William Wilkie, farmer, and his daughter, Isla, and the family dog, Dick, at the front door of Braid farmhouse, *c.* 1919. William Wilkie was tenant farmer at Braid and Comiston. *Courtesy of Miss Isla Wilkie.*

❧ *Left.* This panoramic view, taken from the Braid Hills in 1946, shows Granton Gasworks, the Fife coast, Edinburgh Castle and many of the city centre church spires and domes. On the extreme left of the picture, the two light-coloured sloping roofs belong, on the left, to South Morningside Church (now the Church Centre), and, on the right, to St Matthews Parish Church (now Morningside). To the right of the two churches are Morningside Road, Falcon Avenue and Braid Avenue. In the foreground, the cottages in the bottom right-hand corner also appear in the photograph at the top of this page. Only one house can be seen on what is now Braid Farm Road.
Courtesy of Miss Isla Wilkie.